THE PLACE OF
POETRY

THE PLACE OF
POETRY

Two Centuries of an Art in Crisis

CHRISTOPHER CLAUSEN

THE UNIVERSITY PRESS OF KENTUCKY

Library of Congress Cataloging in Publication Data

Clausen, Christopher, 1942-

The place of poetry.

Includes bibliographical references and index.

1. American poetry—History and criticism.
2. English poetry—19th century—History and criticism.   3. English poetry—20th century—History
and criticism.   4. Literature and society—United
States.   5. Literature and society—Great Britain.
I. Title.

| PS303.C57 | 821'.009 | 80-5172 |
| ISBN 0-8131-1429-2 | | AACR2 |

Scholarly publisher for the Commonwealth,
serving Berea College, Centre College of Kentucky,
Eastern Kentucky University, The Filson Club,
Georgetown College, Kentucky Historical Society,
Kentucky State University, Morehead State University,
Murray State University, Northern Kentucky University,
Transylvania University, University of Kentucky,
University of Louisville, and Western Kentucky University.

Editorial and Sales Offices: Lexington, Kentucky 40506

For Nancy

CONTENTS

ACKNOWLEDGMENTS

Earlier versions of chapters two, four, and six have appeared in the *Georgia Review*. An earlier version of chapter three appeared in the *Sewanee Review* under the title "Tintern Abbey to Little Gidding: The Past Recaptured." Some of the material in chapters five and seven appeared in the *Virginia Quarterly Review* under the title "The Decline of Anglo-American Poetry."

I am grateful to the National Endowment for the Humanities for a summer stipend that enabled me to complete this book. I must also thank Virginia Polytechnic Institute and State University for travel funds that made my research easier, and for secretarial help.

My acknowledgment of debts gratefully incurred would not be complete without mention of Michael L. Campbell, George Core, Russell B. Gill, Stanley W. Lindberg, Wyatt Prunty, James Scoggins, Alison G. Sulloway, and John Taggart, who have helped me to make some chapters better than they would otherwise be, and Wayne C. Booth, whose many kinds of assistance go back many years. My greatest obligation is recognized in the dedication.

ONE

Rhyme or Reason

I was promised on a time
To have reason for my rhyme.
From that time, unto this season,
I received nor rhyme, nor reason.

Edmund Spenser to Queen Elizabeth,
on not receiving a promised gratuity.

Since the end of the eighteenth century, poetry in England (and subsequently in America) has been an art in continual crisis. As its cultural status declined, as its place as a bearer of truth was more and more taken by the sciences, its practitioners made an endless series of revolutions in poetic doctrine while seeking unsuccessfully to make society once again listen to them. This crisis has faced every poet since Wordsworth, and it has never been resolved. The place of poetry in English and American civilization has become more and more peripheral, despite the fact that every major poetic movement since the first generation of Romantics has represented an attempt to gain back lost ground.

This continuity in poetry since the end of the eighteenth century is far more impressive than the breaks between its three conventionally defined periods, Romantic, Victorian, and Modern; for each poetic generation has been primarily occupied with trying to find or make a place for its art in a world that has seemed ever more hostile or indifferent. Each major innovation in English poetry has been an unsuccessful, or at best briefly successful, attempt to assert, either to the culture at large or to a significant minority, the value of poetry itself. Roughly speaking, these attempts have been associated with two opposed assertions: one, that the poetic imagination provides a kind or kinds of truth at least as valuable as anything science can give us; the other, that poetry is not concerned with truth at all and represents an internally self-sufficient system whose justification is entirely esthetic. (Attempts have sometimes been made to combine the two positions by maintaining, in effect, that poetry is like mystical experience and embodies truths that evaporate upon being clearly stated.) Meanwhile the poetic audience, even among intellectuals, has largely vanished.

This book is a critical study of some episodes in the history of modern Anglo-American culture as reflected in the struggles and fortunes of its poets. The essays that make it up are all concerned, in varying ways, with the place of poetry as it has evolved—and declined—during the nineteenth and twentieth centuries. The great Romantics and their successors were all aware (dimly or clearly) that a calamity had occurred in the status and purposes of their art; all tried in a variety of ways to cope with its results, some fruitfully, others less so. Because the crisis of poetry goes to the roots of its nature and purposes, we shall have to consider briefly what poetry is before we can understand what happened to it.

Poetry is that form of discourse in which the line, or whatever oral measure corresponds to it, is a basic unit of sound and meaning. It may be that this definition, although more precise and workable than any other, leaves out something essential—whatever imaginative, emotive, or simply "poetic" qualities are thought to be characteristic of poetry in a deeper sense. The modern critical insistence on seeing poems "as poems" (the phrase is often italicized, as though we were forever in danger of seeing them as something else) immediately raises the question of the relation of poetry to prose, and the further question of whether they embody distinct modes of thought and experience. If form and content are really inseparable, as several recent generations of critics have insisted, then poetic forms ought to embody particular kinds of attitudes and feelings, if not subjects. Nearly everyone assumes that in fact they do so, despite the contrary modern insistence that there are no unpoetic subjects and the historical fact that poems have been written expressing almost every conceivable attitude about almost everything under the sun. And perhaps this last is what we should expect. No one would dream of defining a characteristic set of prose subjects, attitudes, or tones. Poetry has a longer history than prose; why should it be any less various?

When we speak of "poetry," we are inevitably talking about form; form is what distinguishes poetry from prose. Like prose, some poetry is fiction, some is not; some is light, some heavy; some is simply information, although in modern times such poetry is exceptional. Poetry of the last few centuries is usually more compressed and less specialized than prose. Like life's, its regularity does not preclude it from mixing everything together. Nonetheless, it has been assumed almost universally—even though some recent and contemporary poets would dispute it—that there is a further, distinctively "poetic" quality to poetry, and such a presumably irreducible quality has been the basis of most definitions.

The attempt to define poetry has fallen into some disrepute in recent decades; the assumption that it is either so exalted or so nebulous as to defy definition has been widely shared. One recent study of lyric poetry even goes so far as to say—in a footnote—"But, to ask the question again, what makes [a work] a 'poem'? Simply the fact that it can be generally agreed upon that it is a 'poem.'"[1] If we look at some well known accounts, perhaps we shall see why the same author, Gémino H. Abad, refers to the definition of the subject of his book as "a kind of critical *ignis fatuus*." Still, as Emily Dickinson advised, "Better an ignis fatuus / Than no illume at all." At the very least, by examining some famous attempts at definition, we shall get some notion of what people during the last two hundred years or so have thought they were talking about when they argued about the place of poetry in a world whose fundamental knowledge and understanding of itself were derived increasingly from science. Because we are concerned with the last two centuries, my set of definitions begins with Wordsworth: "Poetry is the imaginative expression of strong feeling, usually rhythmical . . . the spontaneous overflow of powerful feelings recollected in tranquillity." This definition is a purely emotional one and sets the tone for other Romantic definitions of poetry, although as we shall see Wordsworth's view of his art was a more ambitious one than these famous words imply.

Next Coleridge: "A poem is that species of composition which is opposed to works of science by proposing for its *immediate* object pleasure, not truth; and from all other species (having this in common with it) it is discriminated by proposing to itself such delight from the whole as is compatible with a distinct gratification from each component part." Such a definition might, of course, include prose fiction, which is in fact subsumed under many older concepts of poetry. In its murkiness, its emphasis on pleasure as opposed to truth, and its invitation to notice matters of structure, Coleridge's definition is clearly an ancestor of twentieth-century literary criticism. He adds, however: "No man was ever yet a great poet, without being at the same time a profound philosopher. For poetry is the blossom and the fragrancy of all human knowledge, human thoughts, human passions, emotions, language."

By the time we get to Poe, the conception of poetry as an art with any intellectual functions at all has become open to question: "I would define the poetry of words as the rhythmical creation of beauty. Its sole arbiter is taste. With the intellect or with the conscience it has only collateral relations. Unless incidentally, it has no concern whatever either with duty or with truth." But Matthew Arnold reasserts, in a half-hearted way, the function of poetry as a bearer of truth, "a criticism of life under the conditions fixed for such a criticism by the laws of poetic truth and beauty."

Emily Dickinson's view of her art is entirely emotional, though expressed in physical terms: "If I read a book and it makes my whole body so cold no fire can ever warm me, I know that it is poetry. If I feel physically as if the top of my head were taken off, I know that it is poetry." Although striking, this definition would not help us to distinguish a poem from a bad hangover. In the early twentieth century Edwin Arlington Robinson tries to smuggle the truth-telling function back in under cover of the emotional: "Poetry is language that tells us, through a more or less emotional reaction, something that cannot be said. All poetry, great or small, does this."

All of these definitions except the second (which is from the *Biographia Literaria,* chapters XIV, XV) are taken from a contemporary handbook for students of literature whose thirteen definitions, none of which is earlier than Wordsworth, all emphasize the emotional elements in poetry.[2] One could, of course, find major poems that would violate any of these definitions, which would, perhaps, only prove the justice of Dr. Johnson's claim that "to circumscribe poetry by a definition will only show the narrowness of the definer."[3]

Far more noteworthy than the variousness of these definitions, however, is their essential agreement that poetry is an art in which intellect and ideas have little place. In her recent book on lyric poetry, the only kind that is much practiced in the twentieth century, Barbara

Hardy declares as a matter of accepted fact: "The lyric does not provide an explanation, judgment or narrative; what it does provide is feeling, alone and without histories or characters. . . . The advantage of lyric poetry comes from its undiluted attention to feeling and feeling alone, and its articulateness in clarifying that feeling."[4] This is not a conception of poetry, lyric or otherwise, that one finds before the nineteenth century; if it were, the major subject of this book—the conflict over whether poetic or scientific discourse was better suited to interpret life and conduct for the modern mind—could scarcely have been possible. If poetry were (or had always been assumed to be) purely emotional, or if it offered nothing more than pleasure, few people would ever have taken it seriously enough to attack it. Nor would it have required any defense, except against that variety of puritan who is opposed to pleasure on principle. It would have been as culturally insignificant as pushpin, to which Jeremy Bentham famously compared it around the same time that Wordsworth was making prophetic claims for it. In fact, the notion of poetry to which all these definitions point is a recent creation, and a consequence of the conflict with science.

A well known traditional definition will show what I mean. It is from Sir Philip Sidney's *Apology for Poetry,* first published in 1595, and for our purposes it has the merit of not having been very original: "Poesy, therefore, is an art of imitation, for so Aristotle termeth it in his word *Mimesis,* that is to say, a representing, counterfeiting, or figuring forth; to speak metaphorically, a speaking picture, with this end, to teach and delight."[5] "To teach and delight"—almost every writer on poetry from ancient times until the end of the eighteenth century assumed these to be the purposes of the art, or indeed of art in general, although poetry had special opportunities and responsibilities because it was articulate. That it *is* a purposive definition is also worthy of note, since some of the more recent definitions I have quoted seem to imply that poetry is not so much a deliberate activity as an involuntary release of emotional pressure, a pure expression of feeling, whose subjects and function for the reader are less important than the relief that creating it affords to its author. For Sidney and his successors, emotion is only a part of poetry, and it is deliberately subordinated to other things. It is the "other things" that brought poetry into collision with philosophy, religion, and—from Sidney's time onward—science.

None of the quoted definitions attempts to circumscribe a special set of poetic *subjects,* not even Sidney's, although Sidney does distinguish three essential varieties of poet more or less according to subject matter—religious, philosophical, and "right" poets who "borrow nothing of what is, hath been, or shall be." Although poetry has rarely been used in modern times merely to convey information, and there are some subjects about which poems have seldom or never been written, it has generally been assumed that the essentially poetic quality lies not in subjects but in the way they are approached. For most of the modern writers quoted above, poetry differs from prose by being more thoroughly emotional, although such a distinction could not possibly survive an examination of the more emotional sorts of prose fiction and autobiography, or of the poetry of Chaucer and Pope. Nor can poetry today be distinguished from prose by its metrical qualities, since free verse has become not merely a variety of verse but the dominant variety. Poetry, in its traditional metrical forms at least, makes use of more of the possibilities of language; it is potentially, and often in fact, more versatile, precise, and concise. Still there is in theory no reason that anything sayable in verse should not be sayable in prose (if at greater length and with less power); and in fact one can find good poems that are as abstract as the most philosophical prose, or good prose that is as connotative, sensuous, allusive, and emotion-laden as the most romantic of poetry.

The significant distinction lies not in the inherent differences between verse and prose but in the characteristic uses to which both have been put since the invention of printing, and to some extent since the art of writing became widespread. Young civilizations are often fascinated by the shapes of words—their rhythms, alliterative possibilities, rhymes, mutations into each other—and create poetry before they create prose. Metaphor is the beginning of thought. In preclassical Greece, in early Anglo-Saxon England, and in other societies at or before the beginnings of literacy, poetry performed tasks for which prose is now almost always used, presumably because meter and alliteration made it easy to remember. Parmenides' philosophy, Hesiod's treatise on farming, and Anglo-Saxon works about medicine were all composed in verse. With wider literacy and the rise of analytic prose, poetry and the imagination inevitably yielded part of their place at the center of culture. At length poetry became a conscious game of words, a form of play that nevertheless at its best was seen to be both serious and important: the most potent expression of truth or falsehood that language was capable of. When verse came to seem more artificial than prose, poets revelled in artifice. No wonder that the Renaissance was fascinated by more and more complicated rules for playing, and at the same time by the question of whether the poetic muse was a true or false prophet. The history of written discourse, at least in western civilization, shows the growing use of prose not merely for information, but for such increasingly specialized subjects as philosophy, theology, and science. In the course of its adaptation to such uses, prose developed increasingly denotative and technical possibilities in its vocabulary—indeed, developed a variety of distinct vocabularies for different uses—while poetry remained unspecialized within an increasingly narrow range of subjects, in which its precision and subtlety made it and still make it unrivalled. Yvor Winters puts the result of this evolution succinctly: "The philosopher or the scientist endeavors as far as may be to employ only the denotative aspect of language; the poet employs the total content," adding that as a result poetry "is the finest medium that we have for the exploration and understanding of the complete human experience."[6]

The laws of language permit statements that reason, revelation, and empiricism all frown on, and poetry sometimes takes advantage of these resources—more often, perhaps, than prose does. (It is no wonder that poets have so often been in trouble with the leaders of established thought.) But as civilization develops, poetry also changes—it becomes more intellectual and philosophical, without losing its original devotion to sound and the imagination. Thus poetry remains in highly civilized ages a bridge between the primitive and the rational, the child and the adult, the emotional and the abstract. As Winters conceives it, the refusal to separate the denotative from the connotative elements of language gives poetry great advantages in the interpretation of human experience, since all experience, when accurately rendered in words, involves both conception and feeling.

When such a high value is set on progress that the best minds would rather repudiate their history than embrace it, however, poetry comes to seem not so much a valued mediator between the elements of our nature as a dangerous anachronism. At two crucial stages in the development of modern civilization, influential thinkers saw the matter in this light. In classical Greece at the coming of age of philosophy, and in Europe on the brink of modern science, the question began to be raised whether it was really worthwhile paying much attention to the ideas and feelings of writers who brought to their task neither philosophical rigor nor scientific discipline. Poetry was neither fully rational nor committed to verifiable fact; it used its powerful rhetorical resources to teach (either through insight or through exhortation), yet its teachings were not subject to any system of validation. It was not just that philosophical or scientific discoveries contradicted some of the things that poets had taught; it was that the whole attitude toward belief itself underwent a gradual change. Instead of a virtue, belief without evidence or rigorous logical support came gradually to seem an intellectual vice. When it did so, the very power of poetic artifice was often seen as a threat to the rule of reason, regardless of the particular assertion the poet happened to be making.

It was Plato who made the first and most powerful case against poets as false prophets, a case whose continuing effect is attested by the fact that Sidney in the sixteenth century and Shelley in the nineteenth wrote answers to it. Indeed, the impact and prophetic force of Plato's attack can best be appreciated in the nineteenth and twentieth centuries, as we shall see in the next chapter. In the seventeenth and eighteenth centuries, he was echoed by men of lesser scope who were trying to prepare the way for science and its domination of the modern mind just as Plato had tried to clear the ground for the philosophical way of life. For Francis Bacon, the "rational soul" has three faculties—memory, imagination, and reason—which produce the three kinds of knowledge—history, poetry, and philosophy. (Philosophy includes science, which is to be the philosophy of the future.) This sensible division does not lead to a relation of equals, however; poetry is for the most part "the dream of learning" since imagination obeys no laws but its own, while philosophy is "the palace of the mind." (History, as the knowledge of particulars, falls somewhere between the dubious teachings of poets and the abstract, theorized knowledge that is philosophy.) Poetry, in short, while too various to be characterized as either virtuous or vicious, is in general the product of credulous ages, and as we advance in reason we ought to outgrow it.[7] This assertion is echoed with greater vehemence by John Locke at the end of the seventeenth century. To Locke (following Hobbes as well as Bacon), figurative language was an "Abuse of Words"; it prevented that clarity and unequivocalness which science and rationalism both depended on. Its use was harmless where the intention was merely to entertain, but its presence in all other contexts served "for nothing else but to insinuate wrong *Ideas,* move the Passions, and thereby mislead the Judgment."[8] The language of the modern scientific world, like its knowledge, was to be denotative, univocal, empirical. Poetry and its rather different attitudes toward language were a major threat to this view of knowledge; therefore poetry, as a major cultural force, would have to be displaced.

As early as the late sixteenth century, decades before Bacon and a century before Locke, Sidney was complaining that poetry, "embraced in all other places, should only find in our time a hard welcome in England," and he takes time "to inquire why England (the mother of excellent minds) should be grown so hard a stepmother to poets" (40). The reasons he traces to the influence of Plato, the reviving suspicion that fiction is falsehood, and the prevalence of bad poets. The nature of his defense is implicit in his definition of poetry, quoted above. In creating his fictions, the poet "nothing affirmeth," says Sidney in a famous phrase, meaning not that the poet has no ideas to teach—Sidney was no theorist of art for art's sake—but rather that the fictions in which they are couched are not put forth as facts. (The modern reader is apt to be surprised that anyone ever thought they were, but Sidney lived in an age when the Puritans, anticipating Locke, were subjecting language to standards of literalness that would eventually work to the advantage of science.) In essence, he defends poetry as a responsible teacher of truth and virtue, both religious and secular. Apart from its style, his peroration might have been written not in the golden age of English poetry but much more recently:

> So that sith the ever-praiseworthy poesy is full of virtue-breeding delightfulness, and void of no gift that ought to be in the noble name of learning; sith the blames laid against it are either false or feeble; sith the cause why it is not esteemed in England is the fault of poet-apes, not poets; sith, lastly, our tongue is most fit

to honour poesy, and to be honoured by poesy; I conjure you all
. . . no more to scorn the sacred mysteries of poesy, no more to
laugh at the name of Poets, as though they were next inheritors
to Fools. (52)

The defense, then, is a conservative one that was to be frequently repeated for at least two centuries: poetry conveys the best and most central teachings of the culture, in the form that is most powerful and at
the same time most enjoyable. This form of defense seems to have been
temporarily successful; as George Watson points out, seventeenth-century critics do not usually complain that poetry is held in low repute.[9]
The religious suspicion of imaginative literature was less important after the Restoration, and the scientific attack had not yet become a
siege.

The attack (which did not come primarily from scientists themselves, who had other things to do), like the scientific revolution itself,
fell upon a world that Lord David Cecil has described, perhaps with
some nostalgic idealization.

Nineteenth-century aesthetes were spiritual hermits; they fled
from the normal world in horror; its interests and its values alike
repelled them as barbarous and philistine. Not so their eighteenth-century forebears. For England, in the eighteenth century, was an integrated society in which people agreed to respect
each other's interests and united to accept similar standards of
value. Often they differed in taste: some liked the town, others
liked the country; some were interested in politics, some in
hunting, some in learning. But the student did not despise the
soldier; the master of foxhounds was proud to quote such Latin
tags as he could remember; and the aesthete was not in the least
disposed to scorn the avocations of normal active life, or to dismiss its standards as valueless.[10]

The place of poetry in such a society may have been modest—more
modest than the Romantics two generations later would have been
willing to accept—but it was also secure. Contrasting Gray's view of
poetry with that of Keats, Cecil continues:

There is nothing transcendental about Gray's view, no vision of art as an expression of ultimate spiritual reality, where Truth is the same as Beauty and Beauty the same as Truth. Poetry to Gray, as to any other sensible eighteenth-century gentleman, was primarily a pleasure: and the poet so far from being the priest of a mystery was a purveyor of pleasure . . . But poetry was useful and even educative: a necessary part of the good life, soothing the passions, civilizing the heart and manners, celebrating beauty and virtue, and, above all, providing an alleviation to the inevitable ills of the human lot. (58)

That the modesty of poets' claims and the security of their cultural position changed simultaneously is no accident; that they changed so rapidly is due to the encroachment of scientific concepts of truth and value during the later eighteenth and early nineteenth centuries. When science was applied to industry, the result was not only the industrial revolution but also the modern idea of progress. Science worked; its power to transform civilization was manifest. To anyone who was optimistic about the new world that was being created after the end of the Napoleonic wars, it must have seemed that English society was at last beginning to repudiate archaic ways of thought, ancient habits of mind that had held civilization back for so long. Now the heirs of Bacon and Locke would have their day. Among those heirs, Thomas Love Peacock and Thomas Babington Macaulay showed just what sort of blasts could be brought to bear on poets in the dawning age of science and steam.

Peacock's "Four Ages of Poetry" (1820) has always been a puzzle to students of early-nineteenth-century literature. Its author had begun his literary career as a poet, then became a successful novelist; a friend of Shelley, he seems an unlikely person to have attacked poetry as an art. On the other hand, his essay is cogent and well thought out. His historical account of poetry's place in civilization is difficult to dismiss, despite the fanciful use of four ages derived from Greek mythology; his account of the displacement of poetry by reason and science is all too accurate. Only at the end, when he criticizes contemporary poets (he calls Wordsworth a "morbid dreamer") and descants on the direction of the times, does he fall into deliberately humorous exaggeration. It is difficult to see how so telling an attack on the place of poetry could have been altogether intended as the joke for which it has often been taken. Regardless of Peacock's intentions, however, the case was one that poets would have to meet, as Shelley realized immediately.

The "ages" of poetry are the age of iron, of gold, of silver, and of brass. The age of iron is that of barbaric society before the invention of writing, when poetry begins in the celebration of heroes. Its sounds fascinate its hearers, and its metrical regularity makes it easy to remember. Because language in its primitive state is flexible, "the poet does no violence to his ideas in subjecting them to the fetters of number." The golden age follows when civilization becomes orderly and writing is invented. Its poetic materials are essentially those of the earlier age of heroes; poetry therefore becomes largely a celebration of the past. New modes of thought as they develop are expressed in verse as well, however: "The whole field of intellect is its own. It has no rivals in history, nor in philosophy, nor in science. It is cultivated by the greatest intellects of the age, and listened to by all the rest. This is the age of Homer, the golden age of poetry. Poetry has now attained its perfection: it has attained the point which it cannot pass."[11]

In the silver age comes "the poetry of civilized life." By this time, prose has developed as a more natural medium for thought and feeling. To express ideas in verse is to do them violence. The poetry of this age is therefore rarely successful. (Peacock thinks of the silver age as including such Latin poets as Virgil, Horace, and Juvenal; in England, it corresponds to the later seventeenth and the eighteenth century.) Such poetry is more polished and intellectual than that of the golden age, more self-conscious. Ultimately, however, poetry is unable to follow the progress of thought because its characteristic uses of language are ill equipped to express complicated or original ideas. From being the leader of ideas, poetry becomes an ever more distant follower.

> Thus the empire of thought is withdrawn from poetry, as the empire of facts had been before. In respect of the latter, the poet of the age of iron celebrates the achievements of his contemporaries; the poet of the age of gold celebrates the heroes of the age of iron; the poet of the age of silver re-casts the poems of the age of gold: we may here see how very slight a ray of historical truth is sufficient to dissipate all the illusions of poetry. (11-12)

Historical truth or not, the decline has a ring of plausibility to it. At this stage, Peacock declares, the range of poetry has been exhausted. There is nothing new for it to do.

That does not mean that poets become extinct, however. Instead, they regress to "the second childhood of poetry." The age of brass is the nineteenth century, the Romantic age, in which by "taking a retrograde stride to the barbarisms and crude traditions of the age of iron," poets attempt "to return to nature and revive the age of gold." In so doing, they show a certain shallow wisdom, for poetry in Peacock's view belongs essentially to uncivilized eras. The Romantic poet (as Peacock caricatures him) is at least being true to the real nature of poetry, though by doing so he demonstrates how grotesque a survival poetry is in the modern world.

> But barbaric manners and supernatural interventions are essential
> to poetry. Either in the scene, or in the time, or in both, it must
> be remote from our ordinary perceptions. While the historian
> and the philosopher [Bacon's disseminators of true knowledge]
> are advancing in, and accelerating, the progress of knowledge,
> the poet is wallowing in the rubbish of departed ignorance, and
> raking up the ashes of dead savages to find gewgaws and rattles
> for the grown babies of the age. (19)

The poet's position in modern civilization is therefore a far cry from the way the eighteenth century thought of it.

> A poet in our times is a semi-barbarian in a civilized community.
> He lives in the days that are past. His ideas, thoughts, feelings,
> associations, are all with barbarous manners, obsolete customs,
> and exploded superstitions. The march of his intellect is like that
> of a crab, backwards. The brighter the light diffused around him
> by the progress of reason, the thicker is the darkness of anti-
> quated barbarism, in which he buries himself like a mole. (20-21)

The prominent place of poetry in education, which was to become a matter of serious contention later in the nineteenth century, is a scandal, for poetry "can never make a philosopher, nor a statesman, nor in any class of life, a useful or rational man. It cannot claim the slightest share in any one of the comforts and utilities of life of which we have witnessed so many and so rapid advances." It survives merely as a plaything from the childhood of the race. Nor is it likely to survive long in the modern age, for Peacock's conclusions lead him to a singularly acute if one-sided forecast of the future of poetry:

> When we consider that the great and permanent interests of human society [i.e., philosophical and scientific advance] become more and more the main spring of intellectual pursuit; that in proportion as they become so, the subordinacy of the ornamental to the useful will be more and more seen and acknowledged; and that therefore the progress of useful art and science, and of moral and political knowledge, will continue more and more to withdraw attention from the frivolous and unconducive, to solid and conducive studies: that therefore the poetical audience will not only continually diminish in the proportion of its number to that of the rest of the reading public, but will also sink lower and lower in the comparison of intellectual acquirement. (23-24)

Romanticism, in short, is the last age of poetry. While the age of brass may last almost indefinitely, the very nature of poetry dooms it to inevitable decline. Unless civilization itself regresses to barbarism, poets will never regain either their audience or their cultural importance.

Shelley's response to this onslaught we shall see in the next chapter. Long before Shelley's *Defence of Poetry* was published, however, the young Macaulay, whose enthusiasm for progress knew no bounds, renewed the attack on poetry and its place in modern life. In an essay entitled "Milton" (1825), he began with some *obiter dicta* on the nature of language that echoed not only Peacock but Locke and Plato as well. "We think that, as civilization advances, poetry almost necessarily declines," he asserted by way of preface. His major reason had to do with the increasing generality of language. Poetry, whose purpose he thought was "to portray, not to dissect," depended on a primitive specificity in words. Thus poetry was much more vulnerable to changes in culture than such arts as painting and sculpture.

> Language, the machine of the poet, is best fitted for his purpose in its rudest state. Nations, like individuals, first perceive, and

then abstract. They advance from particular images to general terms. Hence the vocabulary of an enlightened society is philosophical, that of a half-civilized people is poetical.

This change in the language of men is partly the cause and partly the effect of a corresponding change in the nature of their intellectual operations, of a change by which science gains and poetry loses. Generalization is necessary to the advancement of knowledge; but particularity is indispensable to the creations of the imagination. In proportion as men know more and think more, they look less at individuals and more at classes. They therefore make better theories and worse poems.[12]

Changes in language are not the whole reason for the decline of poetry, however, nor would they lead us to eschew the company of poets or their works. In Macaulay's view, there is something childish about the imagination itself, something which amounts to disease when adults make use of it or claim for it a positive value in the search for truth. "Truth, indeed, is essential to poetry; but it is the truth of madness. The reasonings are just; but the premises are false. . . . Hence of all people children are the most imaginative. They abandon themselves without reserve to every illusion." To write poetry, or even to read it with enjoyment, involves "a certain unsoundness of mind," even "a degree of credulity which almost amounts to a partial and temporary derangement of the intellect" (8). To be a poet in the modern world means unlearning that knowledge which is most valuable, becoming a child again (Macaulay was not one of those who valued the intuitions of childhood), dismantling the intellect itself. Even then, the results are apt to be disappointing, for the whole spirit of the age militates against the creation of great or even good poems. The audience too, as Peacock had said, was declining; progress was rapidly stamping out both poets and their readers. Gone were the days of the prophet and his hearers. "The power which the ancient bards of Wales and Germany exercised over their auditors seems to modern readers almost miraculous. Such feelings are very rare in a civilized community, and most rare among those who participate most in its improvements. They linger longest amongst the peasantry" (9).

Peasants, children, and savages—these were the kinds of people who could produce and appreciate poetry. That Romantic poetry idealized all three could hardly be an accident if the modern adult world offered such stony soil to the seeds of a poetic revival. Macaulay and Peacock might reasonably be accused of exaggerating—the poetic audience in fact remained a large one until the twentieth century—but insofar as the tendencies and ideas they represented helped to furnish modern minds, the age of science would be less receptive to poets and their erratic wisdom than any previous period in history.

It was the promise of science to answer questions and clarify dilemmas that both poetry and religion had addressed for millennia without finality that led to the decline of both in cultural importance. Like philosophy in classical Athens, science seemed to be offering an irresistible certainty to those who would give up figurative or nonempirical ways of interpreting the world and repose their faith in new kinds of speciality. It might not be necessary to abandon poetry (or even religion) altogether, but at the most both would survive as therapy for the emotions, or as entertainment. Near the end of his life, Charles Darwin regretted that he had lost "the higher aesthetic tastes."

> My mind [he wrote in his autobiography] seems to have become a kind of machine for grinding general laws out of large collections of facts. . . . A man with a mind more highly organized or better constituted than mine, would not I suppose have thus suffered; and if I had to live my life again I would have made a rule to read some poetry and listen to some music at least once every week. . . . The loss of these tastes is a loss of happiness, and may possibly be injurious to the intellect, and more probably to the moral character, by enfeebling the emotional part of our nature.[13]

The belief that reason and the imagination are in conflict—held as an article of faith by many poets since Blake's time and by most adversaries of poetry—has been a disaster for poetry, thought, and our entire civilization. Darwin's mind could stand here as a symbol for the modern world he so conspicuously helped to bring about. His complaint is genuinely felt; the loss of what he calls "the higher tastes" is a real loss. And yet it is an entirely emotional one. Other than the reference to the "moral character," which Darwin apparently also regards as purely emotional, there is no suggestion of learning anything from poetry. Its use of language and concepts is an irrelevance; had he continued to read poetry, he would have done so merely as a matter of relaxation and psychological balance. The important affairs of life are all elsewhere. Indeed, the assumption that poetry is valuable as a bearer of truth has become so weak that Darwin need not dispute it, or even show that he is aware of it.

Late in the twentieth century, it is clear that science has not made the world a safer or less mysterious place—quite the contrary—and that its prospects of doing so are remote. Nonetheless, that was what its early enthusiasts expected of it, and in the course of the nineteenth century those expectations became widespread. In such a climate of opinion, poetry as an important interpreter of life came to seem not merely inefficient but, as Plato and Bacon had long before asserted, obsolete. In the 1870s and '80s Thomas Henry Huxley, Darwin's leading disciple, demanded that literary studies should yield their chief place in higher education to science. As we shall see, Matthew Arnold's answer to him made a weak case for the status quo, one that seemed to concede science's primacy as a bearer of reliable knowledge. Such a concession was perhaps inevitable for anyone who accepted the Romantic notion of poetry as emotional self-expression without also accepting the equally Romantic claim that the poetic imagination alone had access to transcendental truths. At a time when scientific discovery was proceeding at a rapid pace, such claims for poetry seemed unconvincing to most thinking people. Today we see science (and science sees itself) in a much less exaggerated light, yet the cultural position of the literary arts is lower than it was a century ago. Part of the reason lies in the ways in which poets and theorists of poetry have responded to the scientific revolution.

In his study of Romantic theory and practice, *The Mirror and the Lamp,* M.H. Abrams distinguishes five varieties of truth that nineteenth-century poets and critics attributed at various times to poetry. "A frequent dialectic procedure," he declares, "was to allow truth to science, but to bespeak a different, and usually an even more weighty and important kind of truth, to poetry." Of the five, three are entirely subjective and have little importance in the cultural debate I am concerned with; they may have helped to maintain the morale of some poets against a hostile environment, but they are too slight to function as arguments. The remaining two, however, go to the heart of poetry's claims to a significant place in modern culture. The first is the proposition that "Poetry is true in that it corresponds to a Reality transcending the world of sense." This assertion and its fate in the nineteenth and twentieth centuries are the subject of my second chapter. The claim is an attractive one for poets to make in a time of spiritual uncertainty, but it did not wear well in the nineteenth century, and I am skeptical about its revival in any form that will convince a large or culturally influential audience. More significant for modern poetry and criticism is Abrams's fourth proposition: "Poetry is true in that it corresponds to concrete experience and integral objects, from which science abstracts qualities for purposes of classification and generalization."[14]

Abrams's wording implies what is clearly true, that science offers a highly abstracted knowledge of the world and self that gives us little help in interpreting the endless ambiguities of life in general or our own choices in particular. Poetry, on such a view, remains an essential form of knowledge because of its unique ability to embody the particular in subtle and powerful form; its lack of generalization is in fact its main advantage. If we are after the truth of moments, situations, relationships, the case of art (and particularly poetry) to elucidate it is a strong one, for such truths are unique and cannot be the subject of theory without being generalized almost out of existence. In a world that takes its truths where it finds them, wishes to be liberated from stock intellectual and emotional responses, and despairs of or distrusts universal Truth (whether religious or scientific), this function of poetry ought to be supremely valued; that it is not so valued in our time may be a complicated accident of cultural history. The poetry of particulars has a long and distinguished history from Blake, who saw in abstraction the imagination's chief enemy, to Whitman, who catalogued the life he saw around him, to William Carlos Williams, who postulated "no ideas but in things." As an ideal, it seemed particularly congenial to democratic and visionary poets, though in lesser hands than Blake's and Whitman's the visionary contemplation of common particulars has often degenerated into the tedious notation of all life's trivia.

Such a view of poetry contrasts sharply with some of the demands that prescientific readers made on the same art. It is worth noticing, for example, Johnson's famous description of the poet's function, placed in the mouth of the sage Imlac in chapter ten of *Rasselas* (1759):

> "The business of a poet is to examine, not the individual, but the species; to remark general properties and large appearances; he does not number the streaks of the tulip, or describe the different shades in the verdure of the forest. He is to exhibit in his portraits of nature such prominent and striking features as recall the original to every mind, and must neglect the minuter discriminations, which one may have remarked and another have neglected, for those characteristics which are alike obvious to vigilance and carelessness."

Here poetry is advised to pursue the very aims that most thinkers of the nineteenth and twentieth centuries have ascribed to scientific theory. It is a notorious fact of literary history that the Romantic poets, Blake most loudly, repudiated this conception of the poet's art. That they and their successors may sometimes have gone too far in the opposite direction is less often pointed out, for if poetry is to function as a form of knowledge useful to most readers, it must generalize more openly than some nineteenth-century and far more twentieth-century poets have been willing to do. In doing so it need not make us feel that it has lost touch with the realities of individual experience, or—the opposite risk—that it has ventured into areas from which the scientific mind might once again properly seek to displace it. Could the science of psychology, for example, tell us anything about grief that would be more important to students of life (as opposed to students of psychology) than the following short poem by Emily Dickinson?

> The Bustle in a House
> The Morning after Death
> Is solemnest of industries
> Enacted upon Earth—
>
> The Sweeping up the Heart
> And putting Love away

We shall not want to use again
Until Eternity.

Could science tell us anything at all in so few words or with such forceful precision? That poetry may be true and important by articulating *typical* situations with this kind of generalized specificity is perhaps one of the less vulnerable claims that may be made for it. We might make a distinction between two kinds of knowing that unfortunately does not exist in English and say that while science is *savoir*—factual and theoretical knowledge about the world, subject to the most formal kinds of verification—poetry is *connaître*, simultaneously the most intimate acquaintance with human experience and its most acute interpretation. It would be rash for an individual or a civilization to dispense willingly with either.

Now more than ever, poets—and critics who wish to make a convincing case for the relevance of poetry to modern readers—need such a formulation of the purposes of their art. Yvor Winters makes a similar point and at the same time laments one tendency in poetry that has helped to reduce its importance in the last two centuries:

The poem . . . differs from the statement of the philosopher or scientist in that it is a fairly complete judgment of an experience: it is not merely a rational statement, but it communicates as well the feeling which the particular rational understanding ought to motivate. It differs from the statement of the writer of imaginative prose, in that the poet's language is more precise and more flexible and hence can accomplish more in little space and accomplish it better. But with the development of romantic theory in the eighteenth, nineteenth, and twentieth centuries, there has been an increasing tendency to suppress the rational in poetry and as far as it may be to isolate the emotional. This tendency makes at best for an incomplete poetry and makes at worst for a very confused poetry.[15]

If this is so, as the series of definitions I quoted at the beginning of this chapter seems to suggest, then poets have contributed mightily to the downfall of their art in a world that values truth and concept more than beauty and emotion. Literature is valuable for a number of reasons, but one of the most important for a civilization is the insights it provides into whatever problems of thought and conduct people in that civilization are most deeply concerned with. Arnold's definition of poetry as a "criticism of life," or Frost's as a "clarification," are more gnomic than they might be, but they do single out the most important demand that readers have made on poetry past and present. The function of poetry, as of the other literary arts, is not simply to depict the inner or outer life but to interpret it; and the cogency, profundity, and universality of the interpretation (both intellectual and emotional) are important criteria, though not the only ones, of the quality of the literary work that embodies it. One of the basic differences between major and minor poetry lies in the greater intellectual ambitiousness of the former. Two of the presuppositions that will guide the rest of this book are that important poetry conveys significant ideas normally intended to apply to the world outside the poem, and that the profundity and coherence of those ideas are a legitimate and important part of the reader's concern, whether he be a Victorian artisan seeking inspiration or a modern professional critic. Nearly all important poets and critics, even Romantic ones, took the intellectual responsibilities of poetry for granted until about the middle of the nineteenth century, and the denial or gradual disregard of those responsibilities has in all probability been one reason for the decline of the poetic audience since that time.

It may seem odd that anyone has ever doubted these innocuous statements. The tendency of criticism since the Esthetic Movement of the nineties, however, has been to see poems as works of music or as paintings, even nonrepresentational paintings, and to examine the tonalities and brushwork with ever-closer attention, ignoring the fact that language, unlike pitch and color, is inherently conceptual. The decline of the rational element in poetry, although perhaps not as precipitate as Winters implies, is an undoubted fact of Romantic and post-Romantic poetry. "Rational" need not mean here "logically demonstrated within the poem"; it stands rather for the intelligible expression of coherent ideas that are meant to be considered on their own merits rather than simply as an element in the poetic structure. The presence of such ideas has not been an important focus of most twentieth-century criticism, to put it mildly. Instead critics, and to a considerable extent poets, have been more concerned with poetic structure as such, and with the expression of feeling. (Indeed, Mr. Abad, whose refusal to define poetry is quoted above, devotes some four hundred pages to an abstruse classification of structures in lyric poetry without ever considering what the purposes of a lyric poem might be.)

The relationship between poem and idea is a vexed question even for those critics who grant that it is an important one, and I shall conclude this chapter by briefly examining some conflicting views of the matter. The first passage, from Matthew Arnold's "Function of Criticism at the Present Time" (1864), contains a notion of the function of ideas in poetry that has been widely shared in the twentieth century, notably by A.O. Lovejoy, who described ideas in literature as "philosophical ideas in dilution":

> The grand work of literary genius is a work of synthesis and exposition, not of analysis and discovery; its gift lies in the faculty of being happily inspired by a certain intellectual and spiritual atmosphere, by a certain order of ideas, when it finds itself in them, of dealing divinely with these ideas, presenting them in the most effective and attractive combinations,—making beautiful works with them, in short.[16]

That this influential formulation does not represent Arnold's last word on the relation of ideas to poetry we shall see in the next chapter; it is, however, a view to which many twentieth-century critics would subscribe without, perhaps, being entirely aware of its ambiguity. If poetry takes its ideas secondhand and turns them into something else, then either the ideas are not (at least to poets and readers of poetry) very important in themselves—mere raw material for poetic transformation—or poetry is little more than an intellectual middleman between the real producers of ideas and the ultimate consumer. By implication (an implication that its author would no doubt have repudiated), the passage deprecates either intellectual originality or poetic creation. By positing an absolute distinction between "beautiful works" and original ideas, however, Arnold also implies that poetry serves a different purpose than other forms of discourse: it has a special function from which it cannot be displaced, although it may be undervalued or ignored in a philistine age.

An opposite view of the relation between ideas and poems is that of George Watson, who, after examining Lovejoy's version of Arnold's theory, declares:

> But two further possibilities need to be considered as well. The first, and less significant of the two, is that poetry might be philosophy in epitome rather than in dilution: more concise, and not always less [more?] obscure, than the philosophical prose which it interprets. . . . The other and much more significant possibility is that the ideas of poets might be simply original. It is surprising that historians of ideas [or, one might add, most literary critics] take so little account of this possibility.

Watson adds that "the principal resistance to admitting the sheer originality of literature . . . probably lies in a widespread misunderstanding concerning what an original idea in literature is like."[17] His chief example is Wordsworth's *Prelude,* which represents a major interpretation of experience that is no less original than most philosophical systems or scientific theories, although it is couched in more modest terms. Watson's conclusion is that if poetry is even occasionally capable of interpreting life with such originality and profundity, its defenders from Arnold to the New Critics do it a disservice by maintaining that its ideas are merely secondhand material for a self-contained esthetic structure.

Lionel Trilling, in "The Meaning of a Literary Idea," points out that the anti-intellectualist view of poetry is contrary to what we know of the history of thought:

> Mr. Eliot, and Mr. Wellek and Mr. Warren—and in general those critics who are zealous in the defense of the autonomy of poetry—prefer to forget the ground which is common to both emotion and thought; they presume ideas to be only the product of formal systems of philosophy, not remembering, at least on the occasion of their argument, that poets too have their effect on the world of thought.

And he adds, as a legitimate demand of intelligent readers:

> We want [poetry] to have—at least when it is appropriate for it to have, which is by no means infrequently—the authority, the cogency, the completeness, the brilliance, the *hardness* of systematic thought.[18]

And, he might have added, the sincerity. Whether we admit it or not, it makes an enormous difference to our reading of poems "as poems" whether what they say, or otherwise convey, is put forth as being true or not, in the ordinary sense of that word. If in reading *The Prelude* we believed that Wordsworth had made up the most important episodes in what is presented as the story of his life, it would drastically change our attitude to what we were reading and, in all probability, weaken our response. Similarly, much of the difficulty for modern readers in taking *Paradise Lost* as Milton intended it is due to the fact that most of us quite simply do not believe that either the events themselves or the interpretation of life is true. The "hardness of systematic thought" is there, however, and because we assume that the poem represents an impressive thinker's deepest beliefs about life we give him full credit for seriousness and sincerity. If it were one day revealed that Milton had simply made use of a Christian mythology in which he did not believe for the sake of creating (in Arnold's words) a "beautiful work," the effect on his reputation would in all probability be disastrous; it would be widely felt by those who had struggled to grasp Milton's alien vision—and rightly felt—that he had been cheating his readers for over three centuries.

The assertion that poetry merely plays with ideas—that it neither originates them, espouses them, nor advocates them—is a recent doctrine, subscribed to by no major poet in English before Wordsworth in defending "Intimations of Immortality" against a charge of heresy; but it has been an element in the twentieth-century critical orthodoxy that has emphasized the "objective" nature of the poem and its distinctness from other forms of discourse. Ronald Crane has put an important consequence of this dogma as well as anyone: "For it is clearly not true in literature, as it presumably is in philosophy, that ambiguities and non sequiturs are always bad; they may be, in fact, precisely what the writer requires if he is to achieve his literary ends."[19] "Literary ends," in such a view, are purely formal; they have nothing to do with anything outside the structure of the poem itself. The New Critical emphasis on the identity between form and content has become a cliché parroted whenever such questions are raised, despite the fact that if content were altogether inseparable from form, paraphrase of a literary work would not be merely unsatisfactory but impossible. As a defense of poetry, this complex of theories has been curiously self-defeating. For the chief complaint against poetry since Bacon's time, and even Plato's, was that it represented muddled thought, mixed with emotion, in an archaic figurative language. The defense that poetry was not really thought at all made it easier still for people educated in the shadow of Macaulay to dismiss as being of little importance in modern civilization.

No one doubts that poetry is older than the kinds of thinking associated with the names of Plato, Aquinas, Spinoza, and Bacon, or that however sophisticated it has made itself, it still bears (like man himself) the marks of its origins in a preliterate age. In its long history, poetry has rarely become as abstract as philosophy, not because its characteristic uses of language are incompatible with logical thinking, but because the most important poets (in English, at least) have usually believed that the clarification of life to which they are committed is best carried on somewhere in the middle ranges of discourse between the wholly abstract and the anecdotal. Whether or not this makes poetry a more effective teacher than philosophy, as Sidney claimed, it certainly suggests a similarity of task, although most major poets have not felt that the task in question was the only purpose of their art. While the desirability of a poetry that treats ideas seriously continues to be a matter of critical debate, it is strange that anyone has ever doubted poetry's abilities in this regard. More than one modern critic has fallen into Macaulay's error about the limits of poetic language. For, as a major twentieth-century poet points out:

> Owing to its superior power as a mnemonic, verse is superior to prose as a medium for didactic instruction. Those who condemn didacticism must disapprove *a fortiori* of didactic prose; in verse, as the Alka-Seltzer advertisements testify, the didactic message

loses half its immodesty. Verse is also certainly the equal of prose as a medium for the lucid exposition of ideas; in skillful hands, the form of the verse can parallel and reinforce the steps of the logic. Indeed, contrary to what most people who have inherited the romantic conception of poetry believe, the danger of argument in verse—Pope's *Essay on Man* is an example—is that the verse makes the ideas *too* clear and distinct, more Cartesian than they really are.[20]

Auden regards the notion that poetry merely plays with ideas as a temptation to poets:

> The reader does not have to share the beliefs expressed in a poem in order to enjoy it. Knowing this, a poet is constantly tempted to make use of an idea or a belief, not because he believes it to be true, but because he sees it has interesting poetic possibilities. It may not, perhaps, be absolutely necessary that he *believe* it, but it is certainly necessary that his emotions be deeply involved, and this they can never be unless, as a man, he takes it more seriously than as a mere poetic convenience. (19)

Despite its ups and downs with philosophy and religion, poetry remained central in western culture from the time of Homer until late in the eighteenth century because its competitors' claims to provide superior insight into reality (no matter how conceived) either were unpersuasive or could become the basis of poetry itself, as in Lucretius and Dante. The prophetic function of the poet might partly involve his submission to reason or revelation, but it was nonetheless widely accepted that poetry was an appropriate medium for civilization's most valued insights and ideas. Since the rise of science to intellectual preeminence, poets have been less able either to show equal claim with scientists to clarify the problems western civilization has (perhaps wrongly) seen as most important, or to incorporate and epitomize the conclusions of their rivals.

Science notwithstanding, the hundred-and-twenty-five-year period from *Lyrical Ballads* to *The Waste Land* managed to embody more of itself—its thoughts and feelings, fears and hopes, beliefs and doubts—

more fully in poetry than any other period since the Renaissance. Even as it did so, however, the audience for poetry was on the verge of becoming both smaller and less serious, as Peacock had predicted. Despite the eminence of Tennyson, Browning, and Longfellow throughout the later nineteenth century, poets were no longer the culturally central figures they had once been; instead of honored prophets, they were on their way to becoming something less than entertainers.

TWO

Poetry as Revelation

"Well, I sort of made it up," said Pooh.
"It isn't Brain," he went on humbly,
"because You Know Why . . .
but it comes to me sometimes."

A.A. Milne, *The House at Pooh Corner*

One important episode in the long decline of religion as a major force in Anglo-American civilization was the attempt, by writers and critics of the nineteenth century, to make art itself the source of religion. The art that lent itself most handily to the purpose was poetry. It had the necessary merit of being articulate, and there was a long tradition stretching back to the Greeks of regarding the poet as, in various senses of the word, a prophet. The view of poetry as original revelation, a more efficacious revelation than Christianity could provide in the modern epoch, seemed to a number of Romantic and Victorian writers both to elevate literature to its proper place and to offer a promising path toward the humanization of the industrializing modern world. Shelley, Carlyle, and Arnold were the most important exponents of this view, Wordsworth its most successful practitioner.[1] Even though Wordsworth shrank from fully identifying poetry with religion, his works were the sacred scriptures of those nineteenth-century readers who put their faith in poetic revelation. Because the religion that had hitherto provided Western civilization with its most fundamental values and view of the world was now faltering under the blows of science and philosophy, poetry would step into its place. Now the poet could truly be a prophet to his civilization; his works would be the new Word, subordinate to no higher authority. Men would live by poetry as they had once, in theory at least, lived by the gospels. "Poetry is the first and last of all knowledge," Wordsworth announced in the 1800 preface to *Lyrical Ballads*—"it is as immortal as the heart of man." Ambiguous though this statement might prove on examination, Sidney and the earlier defenders of "poesy" had never claimed half so much.

The differences that this new conception of the poet's role made to many actual poets are well known. From Wordsworth on, they took themselves seriously in a new way. For the poetic prophecies of the European past had mostly been presentations of the culture's accepted ideas, or a strand of them, in artistic form. If Dante had never lived, the world's literature would be poorer, but the Catholic religion in the fourteenth century would have been exactly the same. While the *Divine Comedy* may have carried home the coherence of medieval Catholicism and some of its meanings to readers with peculiar force—no doubt it has been responsible for an impressive number of conversions through the centuries—it did not create or reveal anything new about that faith. Likewise, if the Catholic religion is entirely false, the literary importance of the *Comedy* is not thereby diminished, as T.S. Eliot took such pains to demonstrate.

Clearly the same is not quite true of the kinds of poetry Wordsworth, his contemporaries, and his Victorian successors wrote when they felt the prophetic mantle descend on their shoulders. If Wordsworth had never written "Tintern Abbey" the religion of nature would have been significantly different, and many people in the nineteenth century (perhaps even in the twentieth) would have held different beliefs about the world. Conversely, those critics who reject the central Romantic assertions about the world have been notoriously unfavorable toward Romantic poetry as poetry, despite or because of their notion that poetry is not prophetic in the Wordsworthian sense and that its truth or falsity is an irrelevance. The appalling fact that such a work as Philip James Bailey's *Festus* (1839) seemed a revelation to several generations of nineteenth-century readers shows the depths to which the notion of prophetic poetry could lead. When revelation (perhaps unavoidably) turns to tract, it becomes easy to understand the post-Victorian reaction against it, to whose origins I shall return.

Nineteenth-century poetry owes much of its character to the fact that the poet who sees his task as original revelation will often be discursive; detachable content will inevitably assume great importance in his work. For Wordsworth and Shelley, imagination is not ingenuity or inventiveness; it is the faculty that finds unity in seeming plurality. Its goal, as Wordsworth says in *The Prelude,* is "great truths." Poets are "Prophets of Nature" charged with bringing closer mankind's day of redemption.

The poetry of such writers will be much less easy to consider in isolation from its messages than the poems of men, like Donne or Dante, for whom poetry as an art does not bear such burdens. Donne's religious poems could be shorter and more compressed than Wordsworth's partly because his readers already knew a great deal about Donne's religion and had plenty of opportunities outside the poem for understanding it. We should not be surprised that the reaction against prophetic poetry later in the nineteenth century led eventually to the hegemony of a critical movement that detached belief altogether from poetry, frequently compared poems to works of music, admired Donne extravagantly, and praised compression and wit above almost all other poetic virtues.

The success of this reaction in twentieth-century poetry and criticism is an indication that, despite appearances, the exaltation of poetry as revelation represented not a lasting increase in its cultural importance, but rather a stage in its decline. Prophetic poetry never fully recovered from Wordsworth's inability to be sure that the unities he found in the world were not simply projections of his wish that reality should be one, and from his consequent failure to write *The Recluse,* the vast prophetic scripture in verse that was intended to crown his career. Where Wordsworth failed, no one else succeeded. Instead of poetry replacing religion, both continued their slide toward a culturally marginal status; both eventually became, as Jay Gatsby said in another context, "just personal." The inheritor of their old position was science. The genuine prophets of the modern age—its definers of values, of the real, and of the image of man himself—would be neither churchmen nor poets; the successors of Wordsworth and Shelley in these matters would be Darwin, Huxley, Einstein, Freud.

Poets realized the overwhelming cultural change that science represented sooner, probably, than any other element in the population—almost certainly before most scientists—and nearly every significant English poet from Wordsworth through Eliot and Auden, regardless of his political or doctrinal views, has been hostile to the cultural and intellectual effects of science. Whereas science is literal-minded, univocal, empirical, impersonal (qualities found frequently in the poetry of the eighteenth century and advocated by Johnson's criticism), poetry in the Romantic age became heavily connotative, intuitive, equivocal, personal, and prophetic. It exalted the childish and the primitive in a way that poetry had rarely done before. The emphasis on the personal naturally led to great variety, but in its general tendencies the poetry of the last one hundred seventy-five years—both before and since the rise of modernism—has been the mirror opposite of what its successive authors saw in science; and even as poetry gradually lost most of the audience it had once possessed, ever higher claims were made for its importance. Although modernism shifted the grounds of those claims somewhat, driving the conception of poetic revelation underground, high claims continue to be made in a world where very few people read poetry at all.

The claim that poetry is superrational has historically been closely related to the charge that it is subrational. It is ironic that the positive qualities Romantic and Victorian critics attributed to poets were so similar to Plato's accusations against poets in *The Republic,* and that his reasons for wishing to keep them out of his state bear such a resemblance to the actual reasons for poetry's decline in importance two and a half millennia later. It is as if, in this case, Plato had been an early philosopher of science seeking to bring about the revolution in a whole civilization's ways of thought that ultimately occurred in the nineteenth century: the substitution of an abstract and general vocabulary for one that is personal, figurative, and concrete; the replacement of intuition and emotion by reason; and above all an epistemology in which the perceiving subject knows itself as separate from the perceived object. A greater contrast with Romantic poetry could hardly be possible; it is after all the split between the self and the world that nineteenth-century poets sought hardest to overcome.

"Plato's target in the poet is precisely those qualities we applaud in him," says the classicist Eric Havelock: "his range, his catholicity, his command of the human emotional register, his intensity and sincerity, and his power to say things that only he can say and reveal things in ourselves that only he can reveal."[2] These qualities led the poet to possess that kind of prophetic influence which in Plato's view was inconsistent with a rational, scientific society. Since the sort of attack Plato made on poetry and its practitioners has mostly been made by implication in the modern world—few of the apostles of science, at least since Macaulay and the first generation of utilitarians, have bothered to attack poetry in any detail—it is worth examining Plato's case to see how its logic applies to the situation of poetry in the nineteenth and twentieth centuries.

Writing in a time when preliterate habits of thought were still prominent, Plato sought to bring about the revolution in the Greek mind that I have described above and found reverence for Homer and later poets standing in his way. Poetry was at the center of Greek education—indeed, it virtually defined the Greek way of life—and in that position it perpetuated the prerational identification of subject with object which Plato thought necessary to abolish if philosophical modes of thought were to become dominant. "The poetic experience," Havelock paraphrases, "is the function of a faculty which is the antithesis of science; it is a condition of opinion which accepts a constant wandering and contradiction in physical reporting; one which is alien to number and to calculation" (239). Poetry uses the language of becoming rather than the language of being; it describes specific and often imaginary events rather than universal forms, and therefore, in Plato's terms, is an imitation of an imitation. Furthermore, the part of the mind to which poetry appeals so powerfully is the least mature part: "the area of the nonrational, of the pathological emotions, the unbridled and fluctuating sentiments with which we feel but never think. When indulged in this way they can weaken and destroy that rational faculty in which alone lies hope of personal salvation and also scientific assurance" (26). As prophecy, poetry led men to feel and do all the wrong things; its combination of power and irrationality made its exclusion from the well-managed state and educational system necessary. "The graduate of the Platonic academy has passed through a rigorous training in mathematics and logic which has equipped him to define the aims of human life in scientific terms and to carry them out in a society which has been reorganised upon scientific lines," Havelock declares (31). System and analysis have triumphed; poetry and figurative ways of thought have necessarily been left behind, as part of the prehistory of the mind. The victory of the abstract—that swearword of so many modern poets—is at hand.

The identification of the poet with the primitive and the childlike, endemic in nineteenth-century literature and criticism, is ambiguous in a way that the modern world is more willing to recognize than the Greeks were. Childlike qualities may be something to outgrow or something to regain; disorder may be either chaos or primal freedom; the loss of spontaneity and oneness with the world may be either praised as intellectual maturity or regretted, the way many of Wordsworth's successors regretted it, as a form of cultural repression. Similarly, the Greeks knew nothing of our positive feelings for primitive cultures and felt, unlike many writers of the nineteenth and twentieth centuries, that they had nothing to learn from the people they called barbarians. The modern mind is far more ambivalent about the value of the preliterate and prerational, whether personal or racial.

Nevertheless, the general tendency of thought since the eighteenth century has been in the directions Plato advocated. The exceptions stand out largely because they are in opposition to the rational, scientific revolution that has in fact taken place. The philosophical consequence of scientific literalism and empiricism seems to be not, as Plato thought, the acceptance of timeless forms, but rather a pragmatic skepticism against which prophecy is forever breaking out in revolt. (Their chief literary consequence is the rise of the novel, which before 1850 had become, according to David Perkins, the dominant literary genre by all criteria except that of critical esteem.) In most ages it is the ordering rather than the anarchic aspects of the poetic imagination that have been emphasized, for in most ages that imagination has worked largely in the service of orthodox ideas. That very ordering, however, when it is not the agent of its culture—or when, as in Plato's case, the culture itself is seen as the creation of primitive impulses that should be outgrown—may have unpredictable and even revolutionary effects. Hence the popular modern conception of the poet as a rebel.

Plato's views on poetry were very much in the minds of the nineteenth-century defenders of poetic revelation. They were also clearly in Jeremy Bentham's mind when he made his famous remarks about poetry and pushpin. Bentham's charges against poetry were twofold: it was, like pushpin, useful only as an amusement; more important, it was dangerous because of its hostility to reason. The first point is utilitarian, the second Platonic. Indeed, Bentham went so far with Plato as to say, "between poetry and truth there is a natural opposition: false morals, fictitious nature." Poets attempt to deceive us; their art depends on "stimulating our passions, and exciting our prejudices." Bentham conceded that on rare occasions there had been philosopher-poets—perhaps he had Lucretius in mind—but he emphasized "the mischiefs which have resulted from this magic art."[3] The fact that he made these assertions without developing them may explain why so few later defenders of poetry had much to say about him. Bentham did not enjoy poetry and thought it of little importance; his principal attack on it is a brief digression in a treatise on rewards and punishments. Not surprisingly, John Stuart Mill was the only important nineteenth-century writer who ever bothered to answer Bentham's views on poetry at any length. It was Plato who had made, not merely the strongest case against the poet as prophet, but the case that seemed to have the most contemporary importance as science's shadow lengthened and poetry became more and more peripheral to the concerns of the modern world, more and more incomprehensible to each generation of platonically educated readers.

When Thomas Love Peacock half-ironically amplified Plato's views on poets in his "Four Ages of Poetry," he prodded Shelley into writing the fullest and most pointed defense of poetic prophecy. In *The Mirror and the Lamp,* M.H. Abrams complains that Shelley "left his sense of humor behind when he launched into his 'Defense of Poetry' in 1821," and that as a result "he never quite escapes the disadvantage of one who responds to raillery with a solemn appeal to the eternal verities." But Shelley knew that poetry in 1821 was in mortal danger of losing its cultural role; behind Peacock's shrewd playfulness lurked not only Plato and Bentham but the more inexorable forces of a revolution in thought. Hence Shelley's earnestness; the appeal to "eternal verities" is an attempt to avert catastrophe. His disadvantage lies in the nature of his age, not in the solemnity of his response.

The result is an argument which at least tries, point by point, to retake those positions that were being overrun. Frequently it is couched in Platonic terminology, as when Shelley declares in his first paragraph that the poetic imagination "has for its objects those forms which are common to universal nature and existence itself." His account of the origins of poetry is consistent with that of Plato; the language of early poets "is vitally metaphorical; that is, it marks the before unapprehended relations of things, and perpetuates their apprehension, until the words which represent them, become through time signs for portions or classes of thoughts instead of pictures of integral thoughts; and then if no new poets should arise to create afresh the associations which have been thus disorganized, language will be dead to all the nobler purposes of human intercourse."[4] In the last two clauses, of course, Shelley departs from Plato and begins to turn the argument toward a Neoplatonic justification of poetry on Platonic premises. Not only do poets keep the language alive, they perform the very function Plato had ascribed to philosophers, that of improving it to the point where it can represent timeless being instead of merely transitory becoming. The delicate act of abstraction is performed not in opposition to poetry, but as part of its evolution. As poetry develops through the ages, the universal element shows forth with ever greater purity. A story, Shelley declares, "is a catalogue of detached facts, which have no other bond of connection than time, place, circumstance, cause, and effect"; a mature poem, on the other hand, "is the creation of actions according to the unchangeable forms of human nature, as existing in the mind of the Creator, which is itself the image of all other minds" (485).

Hence the true poet is simultaneously prophet and philosopher; he "participates in the eternal, the infinite, and the one" as no one not possessed of the poetic imagination can hope to do, and consequently "A poem is the very image of life expressed in its eternal truth" (485). Only the imagination can see into the true relations of things, and only the language of poetry can express those relations adequately. Analysis, whether philosophical or scientific, "regards the relations of things, simply as relations; considering thoughts, not in their integral unity, but as the algebraical representations which conduct to certain results. . . . Reason is to the Imagination as the instrument to the agent" (480). The pleasure through which poetry teaches is not inimical to reason; it is simply the expression of a higher faculty that uses reason in the service of revelation. "The production and assurance of pleasure in this highest sense," Shelley insists, "is true utility. Those who produce and preserve this pleasure are Poets or poetical philosophers" (501-2).

While the phrase "poetical philosophers" is an attempt to heal the rift Plato had posited between primitive and mature modes of thought, Shelley's appeal to "utility" here shows that he is deeply aware of a more modern enemy. Shelley asserts that the rise of science makes poetry all the more important; to ignore or dismiss its timeless significance in the new enthusiasm for scientific progress is to bring on cultural disaster. Science without poetry will lead to a moral relativism, a skeptical empiricism, and a constant chasing after what is merely new. He warns of a future in which the mental world will be denigrated as secondary to the changing forms of matter (the belittling word "psychological" was still an infant in 1821), in which a detached objectivity will be the only intellectual virtue, and in which the one faculty that can make sense of fragmentary discoveries has ceased to be valued. "The cultivation of those sciences, which have enlarged the limits of the empire of man over the external world, has, for want of the poetical faculty, proportionally circumscribed those of the internal world; and man, having enslaved the elements, remains himself a slave" (502-3).

The creative faculty is "the basis of all knowledge," and without it science is no more than the pieces of a puzzle which no one knows how to assemble because no one can remember what it looks like whole. Poetry, then, "is indeed divine. It is at once the center and circumference of knowledge; it is that which comprehends all science, and that to which all science must be referred." So far the language of philosophy; but in his famous conclusion, Shelley returns to the language of prophecy: "Poets are the hierophants of an unapprehended inspiration, the mirrors of the gigantic shadows which futurity casts upon the present; the words which express what they understand not; the trumpets which sing to battle and feel not what they inspire; the influence which is moved not, but moves. Poets are the unacknowledged legislators of the World" (508).

For Shelley, the theory of poetic prophecy could be defended philosophically against both old enemies and new because there was a knowledge to which only the imagination had access and to which only poets could give voice. That knowledge was of "the true and the beautiful," "the eternal, the infinite, and the one." It was the most important knowledge for a man or a civilization to possess, and neither science nor purely rational varieties of philosophy could ever supply it. Therefore poetry's prophetic importance is grounded firmly on a vital task that only poetry can perform. Poets may be "unacknowledged," but that does not make them any the less "legislators." Thus, despite the dangers to civilization that have come from ignoring poetry, Shelley remains confident of his own role and importance as a poet, as well as of poetry in general. This is what might be called the "hard" argument for the poet as prophet. When poets and critics cease to believe as firmly in the importance or existence of an ultimate knowledge that only poetry can provide, their confidence in their own arguments for it will naturally lessen, and so will their persuasiveness in the face of further triumphs by science. After Darwin's *Origin of Species,* when it began to seem that science could explain everything, the argument for the poet's special knowledge of anything in particular came to look very much weaker.

Writing exactly halfway between 1821 and 1859, in the same year when Shelley's uncompleted *Defence* was finally published, Thomas Carlyle had no doubts about the importance of the poet, but was a great deal vaguer about the substance of poetic prophecy. For Carlyle, "The Hero as Poet" succeeds the Hero as Divinity or Prophet as the modern bearer of revelation; far from representing an outdated form of thought and language, the poet has only just come into his own. Nevertheless, Carlyle finds it necessary to insist not only on the poet's importance as prophet, but on the reality of what he prophesies about as well. "Poet and Prophet differ greatly in our loose modern notions of them. . . . Fundamentally indeed they are still the same; in this most important respect especially, That they have penetrated both of them into the sacred mystery of the Universe; what Goethe calls 'the open secret.'"[5]

So far Shelley might have agreed, despite the bombastic vagueness of Carlyle's vocabulary. Immediately a new note is audible, however, which suggests that we have entered a new era in which the very existence of transcendental mysteries for the poet or anyone else to reveal has become a matter of widespread dispute.

"Which is the great secret?" asks one.—"The *open* secret,"— open to all, seen by almost none! That divine mystery, which lies everywhere in all Beings. . . . This divine mystery *is* in all times and in all places; veritably is. In most times and places it is greatly overlooked; and the Universe, definable always in one or the other dialect, as the realised Thought of God, is considered a trivial, inert commonplace matter. (80)

By 1840 it had clearly become more difficult than it was in 1821 to argue for an ultimate reality inaccessible to science; that set of attitudes and assertions loosely grouped under the name of "Romantic religion" had become almost as vulnerable to scientific criticism as traditional Christianity was. Carlyle's case for poetic prophecy is a much cruder and more repetitive one than Shelley's, in part because Carlyle knew much less about the art of poetry, but partly also because the predicament of poetry had grown bleaker. Except for Wordsworth, all the leading Romantics were dead; Tennyson, of whom much would be expected in the way of prophecy, had not yet put in a major appearance. What exactly was it that the poet had to tell us? Carlyle could do little better than repeat himself.

> But now, I say, whoever may forget this divine mystery, the *Vates,* whether Prophet or Poet, has penetrated into it; is a man sent hither to make it more impressively known to us. That always is his message; he is to reveal that to us,—that sacred mystery which he more than others lives ever present with. While others forget it, he knows it. . . . Once more, here is no Hearsay, but a direct Insight and Belief. (80-81)

It is doubtful whether arguments of this sort did much to advance the cause of poetry, although no doubt they instilled a certain vague reverence toward an art of which it was necessary to speak in such mystifying tones. The fact that Carlyle mentioned no English poet more recent than Shakespeare, and that he boiled down the Shakespearean corpus to such a thin and characterless essence, does not strengthen his case for poetry as the bearer of living truth:

> Whoever looks intelligently at this Shakespeare may recognise that he too was a *Prophet,* in his way; of an insight analogous to

the Prophetic, though he took it up in another strain. Nature seemed to this man also divine; *un*speakable, deep as Tophet, high as Heaven. . . . No narrow superstition, harsh asceticism, intolerance, fanatical fierceness or perversion: a Revelation, so far as it goes, that such a thousandfold hidden beauty and divineness dwells in all Nature; which let all men worship as they can! (111)

Insofar as Shakespeare's revelation of "the 'Universal Church' of the Future and of all times" was inadequate, it was because he lacked a sufficiently conscious moral emphasis. Unlike Shelley, Carlyle distinguishes between the good and the beautiful. The first is the province of the prophet *tout court,* the second of the prophetic poet. But the distinction is not absolute; to make it so would disastrously weaken the case for poetry in a society that set such store in morality and had its suspicions about any form of beauty that was not morally improving. For Carlyle the good and the beautiful "run into one another, and cannot be disjoined"; all true prophets are poets, all true poets prophets.

Between the vatic view of poetry and the position that mature civilizations outgrow the imagination, several kinds of compromise were of course possible, and one in particular, devised by a contemporary of Carlyle's, has had far-reaching consequences. John Stuart Mill, who had been raised as a model utilitarian, gave considerable thought to poetry from his earliest years of maturity. In concluding that Bentham had underrated its importance, he proposed a synthesis between its claims and those of science that is fundamental to the anomalous place of poetry in Victorian civilization. Without accepting its prophetic claims, or even its importance as a teacher of ethics, he declared it to be of unique value in "educating the emotions" and so orienting its readers to the world. The claims of the intellectual (as represented by Bentham) and the imaginative (as represented by Coleridge) could be reconciled because they did not really compete with each other; to believe otherwise was to fall into the error of intuitionism. Both forms of discourse were necessary to the adequate development of the psyche.

The object of poetry is confessedly to act upon the emotions; and therein is poetry sufficiently distinguished from what Wordsworth affirms to be its logical opposite; namely, not prose, but matter of fact or science. The one addresses itself to the belief, the other, to the feelings. The one does its work by convincing or persuading, the other by moving. The one acts by presenting a proposition to the understanding, the other by offering interesting objects of contemplation to the sensibilities.[6]

So conceived, poetry might be for nineteenth-century society as a whole what it had been for the young Mill himself, a form of therapy. It kept the inner life on an even keel while the more important business of the world went on elsewhere. Poetry did represent a kind of truth, but its truth was restricted to the emotions:

> Great poets are often proverbially ignorant of life. What they know has come by observation of themselves; they have found there one highly delicate, and sensitive, and refined specimen of human nature, on which the laws of emotion are written in large characters, such as can be read off without much study: and other knowledge of mankind, such as comes to men of the world by outward experience, is not indispensable to them as poets. (8)

In Mill's successors (and even in Mill's own writings at times), this precarious compromise broke down because it denied poetry any intellectual function at all. If science were accepted as the only genuine source of knowledge, then its importance greatly outweighed that of art in a civilization which valued truth above beauty, the outer life above the inner. Indeed, if poetry were no more than therapy and superior entertainment, then it might be made obsolete by the rise of psychology and new forms of diversion. Mill's defense of poetry in the face of utilitarian disapproval was a personal one based on its importance in his own emotional life. Nevertheless, the influence of his attempt to compromise the nineteenth-century debate over its value and purposes is indicated by the fact that his principal successors in this controversy, Matthew Arnold and T.H. Huxley, were by no means as polarized as his predecessors Coleridge and Bentham had been two generations earlier.

That the problem of defining just what it was that poets alone could reveal was not Carlyle's alone—that even a major poet and critic might have no more success in the period when Darwinism was mopping up what was left of natural religion—is all too clear from Arnold's "The Study of Poetry" (1880), the major Victorian defense of what was gradually ceasing to be a popular art. One embarrassment to the defender of poetic prophecy was that in the sixty years since Shelley's time, there had been so little good poetry written that actually fitted the description. Instead of embodying Romantic vision, the best Victorian poetry—including Arnold's own—had been by and large a poetry of paralysis, filled with images of unsuccessful spiritual combat, in which increasingly ignorant armies clashed in an ever darker night. Tennyson, who might have inherited Wordsworth's mantle, had merely inherited the laureateship; in his years of fame those critics who looked for poetic prophecy, including Arnold himself, more and more attacked him for being halfhearted, insincere, and "public"—for being, in fact, the kind of poet the eighteenth century would in many respects have found very congenial. Judged by the prophetic standard, his major works did not come off very well.

Perhaps the only sorts of poetry that could arouse much attention in late-Victorian England were those that either reinforced existing ideas or offered escapist entertainment. In America, where Walt Whitman had appeared as an authentic national prophet, his innovative poems of ordinary life had been mostly ignored in favor of the Harvard professor Longfellow's conventionally "poetic" tales of remote times and places—a decided blow to both democratic and Wordsworthian views about the proper language and subjects of poetry. As a form of culturally important knowledge, poetry was losing its place not only by scientific encroachment but also by what seemed to be the defeatism or abdication of poets themselves. In the very year of Arnold's essay, T.H. Huxley, who had been aggressively advocating the cause of scientific education, delivered an address entitled "Science and Culture" that was deliberately aimed at Arnoldian ideas of literature's preeminence. It was thus as the defender of an embattled tradition that Arnold set himself to restating and updating Shelley's defense of the central importance of poetic revelation.

Like so many Victorian writers, Arnold had felt in the decline of faith both a personal and a deep social loss. It was impossible to go back to Christianity—science and philosophy had seen to that—and something else would have to take its place. Here, as before, was poetry's opportunity. Analytic reason, having gotten us into this situation, could hardly be expected to get us out. The new revelation would have to come from poetry. Hence the famous claim: "More and more mankind will discover that we have to turn to poetry to interpret life for us, to console us, to sustain us. Without poetry our science will appear incomplete; and most of what now passes with us for religion and philosophy will be replaced by poetry."[7] This may seem to be a confident statement of poetry's prophetic role, but it is in fact an argument by default; all the other supports for a religious view of life having fallen, poetry is the only remaining hope. If poetry cannot save us, nothing can. We have come a long way from Shelley, for whom the decline of Christianity was a genuinely liberating opportunity for both poets and non-poets. Arnold sees the spiritual situation as altogether more desperate:

> Our religion, parading evidences such as those on which the popular mind relies now; our philosophy, pluming itself on its reasonings about causation and finite and infinite being; what are they but the shadows and dreams and false shows of knowledge? The day will come when we shall wonder at ourselves for having trusted to them, for having taken them seriously; and the more we perceive their hollowness, the more we shall prize "the breath and finer spirit of knowledge" [Wordsworth's phrase] offered to us by poetry. (2-3)

If poetry is henceforth to be our scripture, it is important to distinguish what is gospel from what is apocryphal, and most of Arnold's essay is devoted to the making of such critical distinctions. Arnold's major criterion for separating the "classical" from the spurious, as every student of English literature knows, is the "high seriousness" (elsewhere "truth and seriousness") that defines the genuine article. The application of such a concept as "high seriousness" is an endlessly debatable procedure, however, and its appearance as a standard for identifying literary works worthy to take the place of religion is not very promising. If the nature of reality is really penetrable by the poetic imagination—if poets can to some extent grasp "that vast *not our-selves* which transcends us"—its revelation ought to be more definite and unmistakable than Arnold's tortuous winnowing would suggest. In fact, the essay never makes clear whether or not there is any particular kind of truth to which poets are uniquely privy. At times, even the later Arnold felt that the "something," however indefinite, was really there; but frequently, in James Benziger's words, "he was an idealist by default only; to be anything else would to him have been intolerable."[8] That the great exemplar of poetic revelation in recent times had been Wordsworth, who was himself so uncertain—even "Tintern Abbey" implies that he found the world "unintelligible" except in rare moments—reinforced Arnold's tendency toward vagueness on the crucial question of just what poetry could reveal to us about reality.

As an argument for the replacement of religion by poetry, "The Study of Poetry" is perilously weak, and Arnold approached the question of poetry's prophetic function again three years later in "Literature and Science," a more pointed answer to Huxley. This time he was in an even more defensive posture, for he was attempting to answer directly Huxley's case for altering the literary basis of education in favor of science. Poetry, for which so much importance had been claimed, might be on the verge of losing the little it had, and Arnold rose to the occasion with an argument that was both more modest and more definite than in his previous essay. Granted, he says, that scientific conceptions of the world are here to stay and that religious belief of any traditional kind is doomed. In this situation, poetry as a "criticism of life" is all the more necessary. "The need of humane letters, as they are truly called, because they serve the paramount desire in men that good should be forever present to them,—the need of humane letters, to establish a relation between the new conceptions, and our instinct for beauty, our instinct for conduct, is only the more visible."[9] Literature must take the place of religion, not in discovering and telling us the secrets of the Universe—that hope is gone—but in "engaging the emotions" for the new knowledge and in helping us to determine our conduct. The great artists of the past have still the "fortifying, and elevating, and quickening, and suggestive power, capable of wonderfully helping us to relate the results of modern science to our need for conduct, our need for beauty." The man who has studied only science is "incomplete"; his knowledge of the nonhuman world may be profound, but his emotional life is undeveloped and his ideas of conduct inadequate.

In this modest view of its functions—modest in comparison with revealing the true nature of the world—poetry is not in competition with science, as Arnold took pains to emphasize. Arnold's conception of poetry as a synthesizer and a humanizing agent in a world whose primary knowledge comes from science is what we might call the "soft" argument for poetry's prophetic function. Instead of exploring realms that only it can penetrate, the poetic imagination will help us emotionally to assimilate the meaning of what we know from other sources. Its province is henceforth to be that of values and qualitative distinctions, a realm from which science is presumably barred by its objectivity. The "soft argument" has been widely influential in the twentieth century (as in I.A. Richards' *Science and Poetry*) and is still frequently made today, but it has neither prevented the decline of literary studies in education—Arnold's immediate purpose—nor convinced many people who are not professional students of literature that the realm of values is best explored through poetry.[10] Like the "hard argument," it has failed to provide a culturally successful defense of poetry against the Platonic criticism that it embodies childish, outdated, and ultimately irrelevant ways of thinking about life.

The problem of the relations between poetry and belief is an endlessly vexed one in modern criticism—T.S. Eliot, after grappling with it for years, concluded that it is "probably quite insoluble"—but by the middle of the nineteenth century there were poets and critics who sought to divorce the two entirely. One motive for this solution was a distaste for the didactic. The term is a tendentious one; one man's prophecy is another man's propaganda. Nevertheless, this position had the merit of removing poetry altogether from competition with science, philosophy, or any other form of discourse that depended on truthfulness. Thus Poe, in "The Poetic Principle" (1850), attacks the notion "that the ultimate object of all Poetry is Truth. . . . *He* must be blind, indeed, who does not perceive the radical and chasmal differences between the truthful and the poetical modes of inculcation."[11] Beauty and truth were not the same thing, as Shelley and Keats had thought, and for Poe the concern of poetry was exclusively with the former: "I would define, in brief, the Poetry of words as *The Rhythmical Creation of Beauty.* Its sole arbiter is Taste. With the Intellect or with the Conscience, it has only collateral relations. Unless incidentally, it has no concern whatever either with Duty or with Truth" (275). Its very beauty might suggest things unstatable and transcendental, but such a delicate revelation could never be subject to the standards of objective accuracy.

The view that poems had, properly speaking, nothing to say about the outer world was eventually to have far-reaching consequences in criticism and in the writing of poetry itself. In some of Poe's successors—Gautier and Wilde are obvious examples—it led to a pseudoreligion in which art was itself the object of religious adoration, rather than a revelation of something beyond itself. The poet might still be a prophet of the subjective, but only to other artists and a few *cognoscenti*; the heathen society outside was not worth trying to convert. When Poe's influence rebounded into English poetry from the French symbolists, the concept of poetry as a self-contained world became an important element in the New Criticism, while T.S. Eliot's authority stood behind the view that poetry is neither prophetic nor "intellectual." In the general reaction against Romantic kinds and conceptions of the poet's art, the theory of poetic revelation ceased by the turn of the century to be upheld by any major poet or critic except on occasion Yeats, whose application of it in *A Vision* and some of his poems was so eccentric and obscure that it seemed to strengthen his opponents' case rather than his own.

The idea of poetry as revelation in pure form, however, is not dead. Perhaps it is even on the verge of a revival, precisely because no form of compromise has managed to save poetry from almost complete cultural displacement. As the residual influence of the New Criticism wanes, and as technology seems to lead us ever nearer the apocalypse, the poet's sense of himself as the one figure—however ignored—who can understand and communicate life in the late twentieth century may possibly be returning. Philosophy and science have not, after all, achieved quite what Plato, Bacon, or Bentham promised. The increasing respectability of myth and prophecy as valid forms of understanding, in the anthropological writings of Lévi-Strauss and in the work of some recent critics, gives the poet a ground to work on with which he may plausibly claim greater familiarity than anyone else.[12] It is true that in "*Ulysses,* Order and Myth," Eliot half a century ago advocated the use of myth in poetry as a way of "making the modern world possible for art"; but for the pre-Christian Eliot the myth was merely usable form, not something to be believed. (That so many readers found *The Waste Land* to be the most prophetic poem since Wordsworth's time was a source of lifelong embarrassment to its author.) The revival of respect for myth as an expression of truth that cannot be expressed in any other way—that is inaccessible to the scientific intellect, in other words—may be pointing the direction toward the restatement of similar aspirations for poetry. In *The Truth and Life of Myth,* a recent portent, Robert Duncan revives the "hard" argument for poetry as revelation, basing it partly on the importance of myth and partly on a religious sense that, despite all the exertions of science and philosophy, the world remains genuinely mysterious. While numerous scientists from Huxley to Einstein have made precisely the same point, perhaps it is becoming possible for the claims of the prophetic imagination to be raised again with greater confidence than in the heyday of scientific discovery.

For Duncan as for Shelley, the world without and the world within, falsely separated by the scientific intellect, are to be grasped truthfully only by the myth-making poetic faculty. Once again, we are faced with something real that only the poet can reveal: "there remains the deepest drive of the artist, a yearning to participate in the primordial reality that challenges the boundaries of convention and the purposes of pedagogy again and again. . . . A mystic cosmogony gives rise to the little world the poet as creator makes."[13] Duncan attacks science for having turned the numinous world into an aggregation of usable abstractions, but the most important object of his wrath—one can hardly use a weaker word—is the timidity of poets since Dryden's time who have delivered "their art over to the consensus of reasonable men" and the modernist critics who have domesticated poetry as a subject for schoolmasters. (Presumably he fully exempts only Blake from the former indictment.) In the post-Renaissance world, "poetry, like the universe of rationalist science, ceases to be primal Creation and becomes a commodity, a material for human uses and self-development"

(58-60). About what I have called the "soft" argument, he has nothing to say; the believer does not use revelation merely to smooth the rough edges of the scientifically formed soul. To enter into poetry, whether as writer or as reader, is a sort of death; we must let ourselves be used and transformed by the reality that is reborn in us. To be possessed by poetry is awesome, a mystical experience in the strictest sense of the term.

Possession was precisely the danger Plato feared most from poetry, and with Duncan's impassioned argument in favor of it we have gone full circle. In a society where poetry was the basis of culture and taught men how to be Greeks, Plato argued for reason, abstraction, an end to myth and magic. Duncan, in a civilization where reason and science have become the only culturally sanctioned approaches to knowledge and behavior, calls for a return to the dominion of myth and symbol, the Homeric age before the fall into the abstract. The reversal has been complete, and it is once more possible to see the antagonists in their extreme forms. Not many contemporary English or American poets go so far as Duncan in their views of poetry or of modern life, but it is possible to see in his book one of the directions which an art that has lost its audience, for the time being at least, might be most likely to follow. Where there is little more to be lost in the way of public importance, there is also little reason to compromise and every inducement to take the highest and most serious view of one's vocation. Whether the very completeness of the "Platonic" victory might eventually beget a new public receptive to poets who made such unyielding claims for their art remains to be seen. In any case, purged of its accommodations with the spirit of a rational and scientific age, poetry in Duncan's vision is once again the mortal enemy of those who substitute the static language of being for the dynamic, living Word of becoming. Story and image are keys to reality, which is mysterious and alive. With the poet now freed from the demands of a society that no longer reads him, poetry is once more a revelation.

THREE

The Land of
Lost Content

Those Pure and Virgin Apprehensions I had from the Womb,
and that Divine Light wherewith I was born,
are the Best unto this Day, wherin
I can see the Universe.
Thomas Traherne, *Meditations*

In the middle of the eighteenth century, Thomas Gray, wistfully surveying the unreflective happiness of childhood, had concluded that "Where ignorance is bliss, 'tis folly to be wise." His successors, flying from an adult world that seemed increasingly confused and without meaning, would soon see—and lavishly celebrate—a higher wisdom where Gray had seen only blissful ignorance. Indeed, for many the uncorrupted child would come to seem (in Wordsworth's phrase) the "best philosopher." Like the hunger for prophecy, the glorification of the child sprang from a sense of deprivation—not just the loss of childhood itself, which became a major poetic subject, but perhaps more profoundly the poet's loss of a clearly defined role in rational, adult society. Finding the world of the adult intelligence increasingly unsatisfactory, poets in the nineteenth century turned more and more to the mind of the child as they imagined and idealized it.[1] In this they had been anticipated by a few earlier figures such as Vaughan and Traherne, but the systematic poetic invention of childhood is a feature of the nineteenth century. In a time when few poets saw science and analytical thought as other than threatening forces, the glorification of the unlettered child was almost inevitable. Once the child was praised for the absence of such learning, it was a short step to the proclamation that he had nothing to learn at all, a Romantic notion which has become so widely diffused today as to pose fundamental problems for education.

Whether or not all of literature is a search for paradise lost (in J.P.

Matthews's tantalizing phrase), it is profoundly true that much of the most important Victorian and twentieth-century English poetry is a search for Wordsworth's childhood. (As against, one might immediately add, John Stuart Mill's.) From "Tintern Abbey" and *The Prelude* onward it is a poetry of loss—loss above all of the spontaneity, spiritual wholeness, and naive energies of childhood. Even Tennyson's presumably more identifiable loss, in the most central of Victorian poems, ultimately resolves itself into the loss of that early wholeness and sense of unselfconscious participation for which "faith," in its Victorian and modern sense, is either a synonym or a substitute. The locus of the search is so often a church, ruined or otherwise, that the association of lost faith with lost childhood becomes unmistakable. The causes and effects of what might be called Tinternambulism are most searchingly examined in the middle of the period by Matthew Arnold, whose poetry is itself, like that of Wordsworth, one of the effects. The search for recovery is superficially led astray by the rise of modernism and the literary impact of the first World War; it continues, however, and in the final work of the greatest twentieth-century English poet it reaches its goal. At the end of "Little Gidding," we have come back to the children and the waterfall at last. Now literature and life can, at least in theory, go on to something else.[2]

In 1798 Wordsworth took his walking tour, and suddenly the dissociation of sensibility loomed before him like the sore thumb of a child too old to suck it. Too old he was, for "Tintern Abbey" identifies three stages of his development—of "progression," we can say with hindsight, away from the sense of internal wholeness and union with the world, toward disintegration and poetic sterility. The first stage, "the coarser pleasures of my boyish days," is now a dim memory of "glad animal movements"; its full treatment comes later in *The Prelude,* and its glorification is not a feature of "Tintern Abbey." It is the second stage, that of the 1793 tour when Wordsworth was a youth of twenty-three, that he looks back upon five years later with what he unconvincingly claims is something other than nostalgia:

> I cannot paint
> What then I was. The sounding cataract
> Haunted me like a passion; the tall rock,

> The mountain, and the deep and gloomy wood,
> Their colors and their forms, were then to me
> An appetite; a feeling and a love,
> That had no need of a remoter charm
> By thought supplied, nor any interest
> Unborrowed from the eye.—That time is past. . . .

This is the time at which nature "was all in all." In the third stage, that of 1798, disintegration has set in: to look at nature is to hear "the still, sad music of humanity" and to feel the celebrated presence. Few readers are inclined to accept Wordsworth's claim that this stage brings more gain than loss. When the highest experience involves three perceptions, the eye is no longer single; in the distance lie Dover Beach and the estranging sea.

"Oh! mystery of man, from what a depth / Proceed thy honours." Early youth for Wordsworth is not quite childhood, but it is certainly prior to the worst forms of adult doubt and self-consciousness, and as such is an object of nostalgia. The middle-aged Wordsworth of *The Prelude,* however, mired in his fourth stage, looked back in his sense of loss past the youth of 1793 to the child of ten or fifteen years earlier:

> I am lost, but see
> In simple childhood something of the base
> On which thy [i.e., man's] greatness stands. . . .
> The days gone by
> Return upon me almost from the dawn
> Of life: the hiding places of man's power
> Open; I would approach them, but they close.
> I see by glimpses now; when age comes on,
> May scarcely see at all; and I would give,
> While yet we may, as far as words can give,
> Substance and life to what I feel, enshrining,
> Such is my hope, the spirit of the Past
> For future restoration. (Book 12, 1850 text)

Here we have the locus classicus of the sorts of loss I have been talking about, and the begining of the search that was to obsess many of Wordsworth's successors.

That it did *not* obsess any of the other major Romantic poets but, in effect, skipped a generation is one of the better reasons for thinking of Wordsworth as the first Victorian poet. It will not do to say that looking backward is an old man's game and that few of the major Romantics lived long enough; only Keats died younger than Wordsworth had been when he wrote "Tintern Abbey." Of course *The Prelude* was tinkered with for many years and was not published until 1850; but we are really talking about a widely shared emotional need to which Wordsworth had given the first and most powerful expressions,[3] not about a line of literary influence as such, although the direct influence of Wordsworth on the Victorians was enormous. When *The Prelude* came out it was, in this sense at least, a poem entirely of its time, not a posthumous relic that had been gathering dust since 1805.

As everybody knows, the other great poem of 1850 was *In Memoriam,* and since Wordsworth had the dramatic sense to die in the same year, the laureateship passed from the mourner of childhood to the mourner of Hallam. That Tennyson is not Wordsworth (and that *In Memoriam* is a different poem from *The Prelude*) goes without saying; when one begins to examine the nature and implications of Tennyson's loss, however, one quickly dispenses with the insufferably good Hallam and begins talking about faith, doubt, division, loss of wholeness and spontaneity—about things, in short, which readers of *The Prelude* recognized very well. For Tennyson, as for Wordsworth, doubt, division, and paralysis are the perils of adult life. In the lives of both poets this kind of adulthood begins with a personal disaster—in Wordsworth's case disillusionment with the French revolution and England's response to it, in Tennyson's the death of Hallam. Their ages at the time of these events were almost identical. While both had written poetry before the great loss, each wrote his first major work—and achieved major fame—as a direct consequence of it. Each came of age as an artist, in short, as a result of the loss which was to be his most important subject, a loss which seemed forever to lie between him and the natural unanalytical openness toward the world that was proof against most forms of division and for which the "faith" with which both poems conclude is a precarious and unsatisfactory substitute, though it is the best that the divided mind can do in a scientific age. *In Memoriam* is also a visit to a church, or rather a series of them;

in Tennyson's famous phrase it begins with a funeral and ends with a wedding, and many sections are set at Somersby rectory.

The major difference lies in the fact that Tennyson's faith, unlike Wordsworth's, involved the belief (or at least hope) in progressive evolution. His emphasis rests on the fact of loss and the ways of overcoming it, not on the preadult sources of those things that have been lost. Indeed, to look back with excessive fondness on the period before such problems arose is to betray a *lack* of faith. If Hallam was a prefiguration of "the crowning race" who will possess perfect power, then it is our duty to look resolutely forward, toward them and toward "the Christ that is to be," not backward, even though the only wholeness we have ever known lies in our early lives.[4] Thus there are surprisingly few references in the poem even to the time when Hallam was alive, and the passages about childhood are mixed. On the one hand, as in Wordsworth, our deepest spiritual feelings are childlike, whether in hope or in despair:

> So runs my dream: but what am I?
>   An infant crying in the night;
>   An infant crying for the light,
> And with no language but a cry.

That crying is better than not crying is confirmed throughout the poem; furthermore, it puts the childlike poet in righteous conflict with more learned but shallower adults:

> Let him, the wiser man who springs
>   Hereafter, up from childhood shape
>   His action like the greater ape,
> But I was *born* to other things.

The famous "I have felt" is a similarly Wordsworthian response to the analytical coldness of an all-too-grown-up world.

On the other hand, Hallam is largely praised as an adult who has been through it.

> He fought his doubts and gathered strength,
>   He would not make his judgment blind,
>   He faced the spectres of the mind
> And laid them: thus he came at length

> To find a stronger faith his own,
>   And Power was with him in the night.

Wordsworthian phrase! Hallam's memory is most valuable as a model and inspiration: this is where we should, and shall, go from our present state of suffering and paralytic doubt. Where we were *before* that state is largely irrelevant; psychologically and chronologically the way lies forward rather than back. Indeed, behind us is a past that is far from wholly idyllic; because Tennyson sees it in evolutionary rather than solely personal terms, it contains not only the child but also the tiger and the ape. Nature did in fact betray the heart that loved her—red in tooth and claw, she betrayed a whole generation of Tennyson's contemporaries, as Joseph Warren Beach makes clear.[5] A Tennysonian child shows his spiritual superiority by crying for the light (and, at best, "crying, knows his father near"). A Wordsworthian child has no need to cry at all, unless at the prospect of growing up.

For Tennyson, then, the man of the future rather than the child of the past is to be our icon. The "faith that comes of self-control" is probably incompatible with the undisciplined spontaneity of childhood, even though it is in so many ways an attempt to recover that state. Self-control inherently involves a split in the self; it is by definition inimical to wholeness, childlike or otherwise. In the interests of resolving the dilemma of division, Tennyson, like many Victorians, forces himself more deeply into it by moral and intellectual imperatives. In the major poetry of the nineteenth century we will find no really effective solution to this double bind. Tennyson is no more confident of his own solutions than Wordsworth is that maturity gives more than it takes away; even at the climax of *In Memoriam,* when "the living soul was flashed on mine," his reassuring trance is soon "cancelled, stricken through with doubt." Like Wordsworth, Tennyson is a poet of mid-passage between two worlds, one lost forever, the other lying in an uncertain future. While Wordsworth is most memorable when he renders what has been lost, however, what the reader takes from Tennyson is most of all the shock of loss itself, and the restless if vague apprehension of a far-off apocalyptic event in which all that has been lost, and more, will be restored.

Even such minimal assurance was more than Matthew Arnold felt justified in hoping for. It is well known that Arnold had a low opinion

of Tennyson's poetic honesty and thought his elevation to the laureateship an unfortunate exchange. Arnold's *Empedocles on Etna* (1852),
in which the protagonist commits suicide, might seem a sufficiently
blunt rejoinder to the tradition of shallow optimism that Arnold saw
Tennyson as representing; but as it is set in classical times, it does not
really belong with the poems of nostalgia that we have been looking
at. "Stanzas from the Grande Chartreuse" (1855), however, represents
one of the low points of pessimistic autobiographical recollection.
Childhood and faith are gone, and there is scant expectation that anything will take their place in the foreseeable future.

> For rigorous teachers seized my youth,
> And purged its faith, and trimm'd its fire,
> Show'd me the high, white star of Truth,
> There bade me gaze, and there aspire.

Even to visit a site symbolic of the old faith is a sort of betrayal of those
"masters of the mind" who undid the spirit, and Arnold hastens to
apologize: he comes not to renew his faded Christianity,

> But as, on some far northern strand,
> Thinking of his own gods, a Greek
> In pity and mournful awe might stand
> Before some fallen runic stone—
> For both were faiths, and both are gone.

(Once again Arnold's instincts are with Empedocles rather than Calli-
cles.) The racial past is, as in Tennyson, one of struggle toward the
light; but in this case the issue of the struggle is very doubtful and the
world of the supermen "powerless to be born."

> For what avail'd it, all the noise
> And outcry of the former men?—
> Say, have their sons achieved more joys,
> Say, is life lighter now than then?
> The sufferers died, they left their pain—
> The pangs which tortured them remain.

The great man of the future is a phantom; Thomas Arnold, unlike Hallam, does not point the way out of his commemorator's dilemma. The higher age *may* come, but if so it will be long after this generation has passed on. "Sons of the world, oh, speed those years; / But, while we wait, allow our tears!"

Meanwhile Arnold and those he speaks for sit in their paralysis, having lost their childhood and failed to become men of action because there is nothing left within or outside them to impel action. "We are like children rear'd in shade / Beneath some old-world abbey wall." The call to action comes too late; the banners and the bugles are not for these bastard offspring of Wordsworth and Bentham.[6] It is as if angels with swords blocked not only the return to Eden but the pathway to the future. There is only one answer the "children" of the mid-nineteenth century are capable of giving: "Pass, banners, pass, and bugles, cease; / And leave our desert to its peace!" When it is not a desert, the world for Arnold is a volcano, a darkling plain, an estranging sea. It is full of churches that no longer inspire—Rugby Chapel, Haworth, Broce, the Grande Chartreuse. Nature, like culture, has betrayed its worshippers; neither civilization nor the natural world offers any scope for the adult mind to act without the fatal division. The loss of childhood is a loss not merely of spontaneity, wholeness, and participation: it is equally a loss of illusions; and the hope that we may either go back or, in the foreseeable future, go forward is just one more illusion. The dialogue of the mind with itself has become a series of lectures endlessly repeated.

One consequence of the assimilation of science by the literary mind later in the century was perhaps that poems got shorter. When everyone has been through the same loss of faith, a representative number of spiritual autobiographies in verse is sufficient; at a certain point the better poets leave off retelling a story that is depressingly similar to so many others. They do not, however, abandon their obsession with faith and childhood. What they do instead is to write episodes rather than histories. The three leading English poets of the later Victorian period are Hopkins, Hardy, and Housman. Of the three Hopkins shows most purely the nostalgia for childhood and its closeness to nature—in poems like "Spring and Fall" and "The Handsome Heart"—

but because of his Roman Catholicism he does not associate growing up with the loss of spiritual wholeness in quite the way that I have been examining. In "Spring" he comes close—he advises Christ: "Have, get, before it cloy, / Before it cloud, Christ, lord, and sour with sinning, / Innocent mind and Mayday in girl and boy." Wordsworthian children though they are, however, they are to be redeemed through Christ rather than suspended in childhood. Christian adulthood is an improvement upon childish spontaneity. Wordsworth of course had made the same point, but with a notable lack of conviction. Hopkins is a much clearer thinker and a much more convinced Christian, if also a more tortured man, and the reader is only occasionally struck by a seeming disproportion between the vivid attractiveness of his children and the abstractness of what they are expected to become.

With Hardy and Housman there is no such anomaly. Sadness and loss are the most conspicuous themes in practically all the poetry of both men, and that loss is very often associated with both childhood and faith. Both had pious mothers, and churches figure prominently in the reminiscences of these two outspoken unbelievers. Hardy attended church services frequently throughout his life, while Housman continued in maturity to admire the high-church Anglicanism in which he no longer believed. Hardy spent part of his professional life as a restorer of church buildings, which led him to couple the jaundiced eye of the architect with that of the Wessex poet and novelist when he examined the facades and supporting structures of faith. The neutral observations in the last stanza of "A Cathedral Facade at Midnight" (1897) suggest an intelligent but uninvolved foreman of a wrecking crew:

> A frail moan from the martyred saints there set
> Mid others of the erection
> Against the breeze, seemed sighings of regret
> At the ancient faith's rejection
> Under the sure, unhasting, steady stress
> Of Reason's movement, making meaningless
> The coded creeds of old-time godliness.

The neutrality, however, is unusual in Hardy. His characteristic tone is displayed much more typically in such a poem as "Afternoon Service at Mellstock (Circa 1850)." Here the sense of looking backward (from about 1914) is apparent even in the title; in 1850 Hardy was ten, and Mellstock is his childhood Stinsford. The congregation stands in the pews on an afternoon of "drowsy calm" and sings psalms, which not surprisingly fail to hold the children's attention. As Wordsworth could have predicted,

> We watched the elms, we watched the rooks,
> The clouds upon the breeze,
> Between the whiles of glancing at our books,
> And swaying like the trees.

So far this is merely the staple of most novels about children. Even Alice behaved the same way on the river-bank before falling asleep. What changes matters is the reversal in the last stanza, where nostalgia joins the freshness of the child's perceptions with the stale faith that is boring him and makes them a single object of wistful retrospection:

> So mindless were those outpourings!—
> Though I am not aware
> That I have gained by subtle thought on things
> Since we stood psalming there.

The culmination of Hardyesque nostalgia is "The Oxen" (1915), a poem so emotionally unambiguous that it requires little comment. In it the poet looks back from old age on the simplicity of his rural childhood, in which it never occurred to anyone to doubt that oxen knelt at midnight on Christmas Eve.

> So fair a fancy few would weave
> In these years! Yet, I feel,
> If someone said on Christmas Eve,
> "Come; see the oxen kneel,
>
> "In the lonely barton by yonder coomb
> Our childhood used to know,"
> I should go with him in the gloom,
> Hoping it might be so.

It would be accurate to call this hoped-for scene the unrestored archetypal church of the imagination. The misfortune of Hardy and his generation was that the gloom had merely thickened; neither Christ nor Wordsworth came a second time to restore what had been lost. Too well informed to be optimistic in their unbelief, too honest to accept the vague affirmations of a Tennyson, they were reduced to exercising their emotions in pure nostalgia, wishing that time might have ceased before adulthood and Darwin robbed them of both ignorant childhood certainty and anything that might have taken its place.

Yet there was no going back, either for the poet or for his society; that they knew only too well. Whether in Dorset or in Shropshire, the West of England landscape itself seemed to mock them as an unattainable vision of peace and wholeness that they had left behind. Housman asked in "Into My Heart" (1896):

> Into my heart an air that kills
>   From yon far country blows:
> What are those blue remembered hills,
>   What spires, what farms are those?

The answer will be familiar enough at this point.

> That is the land of lost content,
>   I see it shining plain,
> The happy highways where I went
>   And cannot come again.

For Wordsworth it was at least possible, after five years, to return to Tintern Abbey as an adult and restore oneself in the valley of the Wye, even if the experience was not quite what it had been the first time. For his successors the roads are strictly one-way, and they lead past Dover Beach to the Waste Land. The distant landscapes of childhood have ceased to be a living comfort; perhaps by the nineties they have ceased even to be Darwinian battlegrounds. They have become a mirage.

As a major poet T.S. Eliot began in the Waste Land and ended at Little Gidding. That both places are associated with chapels is no accident: even in the depths of the tradition we have been talking about, the way out is symbolized for believers and unbelievers alike by religious buildings, real or legendary. Since it is in Eliot's later work that major English poetry emerges from its fixation on lost childhood and one kind of spiritual paralysis, we naturally look for reasons that will explain his ability to reverse or (better) to complete the journey that had begun at Tintern Abbey. In *The Waste Land* (1922) there is already a spiritual prescription for modern man: give, sympathize, control. It is not until his culminating work twenty years later that we see fully the meaning and fruits of this advice.

"Burnt Norton" (1935), the first of the *Four Quartets,* begins with the observation, today almost hackneyed from frequent quotation, that "Time present and time past / Are both perhaps present in time future, / And time future contained in time past." In our context this is a pregnant assertion, though its possible meanings are not clarified at this stage of the quartets. At least it raises the possibility that the past to which we look back nostalgically may be fulfilled in some future which is neither visionary nor unbearably distant. That past is "our first world" of leaves and roses and children's voices; but there is something amiss in it, and we cannot stay. The roses, as one might equally say of Wordsworth's performing daffodils, "had the look of flowers that are looked at." Their naturalness, and our own insofar as we *try* to be childlike, is deceptive.

> Then a cloud passed, and the pool was empty.
> Go, said the bird, for the leaves were full of children,
> Hidden excitedly, containing laughter.
> Go, go, go, said the bird: human kind
> Cannot bear very much reality.

What follows is adult life, a life of doubts and evasions. It contains at every point the possibility of transcendence, but only if we are willing to face reality. (What that means is also less than clear at this point.) Meanwhile, like Eliot's predecessors, we are left with spots of time, flashes of shame and nostalgia:

> Sudden in a shaft of sunlight
> Even while the dust moves

There rises the hidden laughter
Of children in the foliage
Quick now, here, now, always—
Ridiculous the waste sad time
Stretching before and after.

The pilgrimage to Little Gidding (1942) is clearly a voyage of recovery, but it is not made in the eager expectant frame of mind that one might anticipate. This is partly because spiritual purposes are never quite clear to those for whom or in whom they are accomplished, nor are they ever carried out in precisely the way one intends. The egotism that leads us to suppose we are either of great importance or in control of our own lives is one of the things we must lose in order to find ourselves anew.

And what you thought you came for
Is only a shell, a husk of meaning
From which the purpose breaks only when it is fulfilled
If at all. Either you had no purpose
Or the purpose is beyond the end you figured
And is altered in fulfillment.

There is no comfort for the egotistical imagination here. We are reminded of several things about Wordsworth and children. First, Wordsworth went to Tintern Abbey initially as a refuge from traumas connected with the French revolution. He described himself as "more like a man / Flying from something that he dreads, than one / Who sought the thing he loved." The purpose was refuge and, on the second trip, a slightly self-indulgent revisiting. Second, and equally important, Eliot's is a more genuinely childlike position than anything we have seen so far. For the most striking fact about children is not that they are innocent but that they are helpless: like poets, perhaps, they have little control over their own lives or purposes. To Wordsworth, being childlike meant something quite different from allowing oneself to be controlled by events not of one's own making, or by the will of another. But Wordsworth, as Eliot might have reminded him, was not the first to suggest that those in spiritual difficulty should become as little children. Eliot's pilgrimage is dominated above all by a discipline that excludes sentimentality and self-assertion. Unlike, say, Wordsworth's or Arnold's journeys, it is undertaken neither as an escape nor as a form of indulgence, but as a duty.

> You are not here to verify,
> Instruct yourself, or inform curiosity
> Or carry report. You are here to kneel
> Where prayer has been valid.

One thing that never occurred to Wordsworth at Tintern Abbey, or to Arnold at the Grande Chartreuse, was to pray.

Furthermore the rejection of history, which had seemed such a promising route for the return to spontaneity and spiritual freedom, is a dead end. "Little Gidding" is, unlike "Tintern Abbey," both a war poem and a meditation on history. The poet reflects not only about the bombing of London, in which he is involved to a small degree, but about the seventeenth-century community at Little Gidding and the civil war in which it achieved its moment of fame. The way to deal with history is not to flee from it but to open oneself to all of its crises and participants without refighting its battles (the royalist and Anglo-Catholic, insofar as they are partisan roles, will have to go). History, like life at any stage, "is a pattern / Of timeless moments." Thus analyzed and accepted, nostaliga becomes something other than itself: it too is redeemed in a larger pattern.

> This is the use of memory:
> For liberation—not less of love but expanding
> Of love beyond desire, and so liberation
> From the future as well as the past.

Desire too must go—not only the desire for wealth, fame, comfort, but also the desire for liberation itself, peace, wholeness, indeed the achievement of any of our own purposes whatsoever.

That this austere, almost medieval form of self-denial is unlike anything proposed or practised by any of our other poets except Hopkins is obvious. That in it lies, for Eliot, our only salvation is evident from all of his major works. "Little Gidding" is in this as in other senses his masterwork, and it is not surprising that after it he wrote virtually no more poems. Yet the reward that the "classicist" offers us at the end of this most romantic of nineteenth-century searches would have made Wordsworth and most of his successors nod their heads. It is, in truth, the achievement of their quest and the way out of their personal and poetic dilemma, even though the disciplines by which it is achieved are alien to all of them: "And the end of all our exploring / Will be to arrive where we started / And know the place for the first time." We shall know it as only adults can know, but we shall be at home in it as only children and those who have given up the desire that their desires should rule can be at home anywhere. The waterfall is hidden but audible once more; the children, "Not known, because not looked for / But heard, half-heard, in the stillness / Between two waves of the sea."

The sea still thunders, but no longer on Dover Beach; the children are there in us so long as we are not primarily concerned with seeing them. And the lost simplicity is restored through what seems the driest and most antiquated of paradoxes—the discipline of further loss. The end of the quest, of course, is transfigured in such a way that the restoration of childhood wholeness is only part of the reward; as no child would be surprised to learn, it fits into a new and unexpected pattern which literarily is Eliot's rather than Wordsworth's and spiritually is external to any thinker. Perhaps it really is true that all literary and spiritual movements are fulfilled by their opposites. More likely, though, the original problem had been somewhat misconceived by poets and their commentators. After paying Wordsworth and his heirs their due for anguish and (often) honesty, one has an obligation to recognize that their difficulties stemmed at least partly from an egotistical unwillingness to see faith and freedom as anything but possessions which they had had and lost and would steadfastly refuse to recognize in any but reassuringly dead forms. It is this refusal above all that Eliot, attentive student of Dante and the aged Yeats, definitively disowns.

Philip Larkin's "Church Going" (1955) makes an appropriate coda to this lengthy episode in English poetry. It is the product of a period and a movement that eschew any concern with such transcendently universal themes. In it a touring cyclist stops to visit a church along his route. He removes his cycle-clips "in awkward reverence" and examines the interior with ostentatious ignorance. "Here endeth," he announces loudly from the lectern, and then is embarrassed by the echoes of his voice. Signing the visitors' book and donating "an Irish sixpence," he departs, reflecting that "the place was not worth stopping for."

> Yet stop I did: in fact I often do,
> And always end much at a loss like this,
> Wondering what to look for.

Not only is the kind of search that so desperately engaged Wordsworth's successors a thing of the past; the very thing searched for has been forgotten, so that the educated and sensitive visitor wanders through and around the church in reverent bafflement. His interest is merely antiquarian, although he is aware that at some time in the dim past churches (like poetry) had a function about which it is appropriate to be respectful. Farther than this he cannot go; there is no anguish, no sense of loss, merely a mild and confused curiosity. "I wonder who / Will be the last, the very last, to seek / This place for what it was; one of the crew / That tap and jot and know what rood-lofts were?" In notable contrast to Arnold and Eliot in particular, Larkin (it would be condescending to speak of a *persona* here) pays tribute to those who built the church and worshipped there, yet shows no sense of strain or involvement. The building is not in the least haunted for him, merely old. "It pleases me to stand in silence here," he declares; but his reasons are those of the anthropologist who has accidentally happened upon a minor shrine of a dead civilization. Here is the last stanza:

> A serious house on serious earth it is,
> In whose blent air all our compulsions meet,
> Are recognized, and robed as destinies.
> And that much never can be obsolete,
> Since someone will forever be surprising
> A hunger in himself to be more serious,

And gravitating with it to this ground,
Which, he once heard, was proper to grow wise in,
If only that so many dead lie round.

The glib and patronizing earnestness of this tribute marks the end of poetic churchgoing in any of the senses I have been talking about. There is in it no struggle, no tension, and only the mildest form of nostalgia. No trace survives of Arnold's self-reproach in the "living tomb," of Hardy "hoping it might be so," of Eliot's midwinter spring. The sense of lost content has itself been lost—either because unbelief and fragmentation have ceased to seem unnatural or because the mind has given up holding dialogue with itself—and we are surrounded by the peace of the graveyard. The dead have buried their dead.

FOUR

The Palgrave Version

His art-criticisms helped to make the *Saturday Review*
a terror to the British artist. His literary taste, condensed
into the "Golden Treasury," helped Adams to more literary
education than he ever got from any taste of his own.
The Education of Henry Adams

The period from about 1870—that date which marks a break in so
many strands of cultural and intellectual history—until a few years after the death of Yeats in 1939 was a time of brilliance in the English
short poem, or lyric,[1] unmatched by any except perhaps the Renaissance. Hopkins, Housman, Hardy, Yeats himself, the early Dylan
Thomas, and a host of distinguished lesser names—in America, Emily
Dickinson and Robert Frost: the achievement is especially striking
when one considers that it came to fruition in a series of decades (1880
to 1910) often regarded as a mere hiatus between the major Victorians
and the modernists. The poets I have mentioned were not, of course,
consciously awaiting that change in human nature which Virginia
Woolf ascribed to the year 1910; indeed, with the exception of Hopkins and Emily Dickinson, who both died before the turn of the century, and of Thomas, who was born in 1914, they all either ignored or
actively opposed most features of what has come to be known as the
modernist revolution in poetry.

They were, however, conscious that what they were doing was not
quite what their immediate poetic predecessors had done. It was not
only the innovative Hopkins who was aware of a break with the cen-
tral-Victorian past; to all of the poets I am talking about, the art of poetry meant something quite different from what it had meant to Tennyson or Browning a few years earlier, let alone to Wordsworth or
Coleridge. The most striking symptom of the difference is, quite simply, the length of the poems they wrote. Gone, or at least greatly
weakened, was the aspiration to write the portentous book-length

work. Excluding plays in verse, none of the poets I have listed wrote anything as long as *The Prelude, In Memoriam,* or *Idylls of the King,* still less *The Ring and the Book.* Their emphasis was on the lyric poem, so much so that Hopkins even insisted that his longest and perhaps most didactic work, "The Wreck of the *Deutschland,*" was primarily lyrical.

The prestige of the lyric as a major genre, in eclipse for centuries, had reemerged with extraordinary strength and speed, a fact of which at least one major figure was aware. As Yeats put it in a broadcast of 1936: "The period from the death of Tennyson until the present moment [he chose to overlook Hopkins and Emily Dickinson] has, it seems, more good lyric poets than any similar period since the seventeenth century—no great overpowering figures, but many poets who have written some three or four lyrics apiece which may be permanent in our literature."[2] That Yeats was understating the case is evident today, not only because figures like Hardy and Yeats himself look bigger than they used to, but also because we can now look back on an entire century in which the longer, more public genres of poetry have been moribund. Gone from the mainstream of literature are the poetic autobiography, the extended elegy, the philosophical meditation in verse, the long satirical poem. Prose fiction has largely replaced narrative verse; the lyric has largely replaced all other kinds. With rare exceptions, the question of whether a contemporary poem is a lyric or not is meaningless. On the one hand, there is nothing much else for it to be. On the other, by virtue of its sudden and complete triumph the lyric has become far more varied and versatile than it was in the days when other poetic forms led a healthy existence.

How and why did this rapid, drastic change in poetic attitudes come about? Why are Tennyson's major poems so long and public, Yeats's so short and comparatively personal? The importance of magazines as a medium for poetic publication seems to be a consequence, not a cause of this change; in any case, there is no reason why magazines should not publish long poems (they serialized novels, after all) if their readers want them to. Nor can we say that poems got shorter because the public's interest in poetry declined. While the cultural influence of poetry was past its peak by the 1870s, volumes by well known poets continued to make large profits for both authors and publishers. There is no economic reason that will explain why the best poets suddenly were writers of short poems rather than long ones. The short story, after all, never superseded the novel, either in good times or in bad. Since the lyric poem did supersede the long poem, it is clear that readers must suddenly have wanted to read lyrics and poets to write them.

A large part of the immediate explanation for this shift in taste lies in the publication of the most important anthology in English literary history, Francis Turner Palgrave's *Golden Treasury of the Best Songs and Lyrical Poems in the English Language.* The *Golden Treasury* is the one anthology everyone has heard of. Dedicated to Tennyson, it first appeared as a pocket-sized quarto in the summer of 1861 and was an immediate success. As Palgrave modestly wrote to the dedicatee some months after the book's publication, "It sells well and seems not only to give pleasure, but to arouse thoughts and discussion about poetry, which I regard as the *causa finalis* of such a book."[3] It did far more than that. In fact it established, retroactively and for the future, the tradition of the English lyric. It did so deliberately and carefully, for Palgrave, a thirty-seven-year-old art critic and employee of the Education Department, the son of a distinguished historian, clearly intended nothing less than to set a standard for English poetry. Poetry in its essential and highest form was lyric poetry; lyrical "has been here held essentially to imply that each Poem shall turn on some single thought, feeling, or situation."[4] From these simple foundations Palgrave erected a rather more complicated structure, as we shall see; but much of its power and durability stem from its seeming obviousness. Indeed, that its major assumptions—the superior poeticalness of lyric verse, the distaste for the heavily didactic and the overdecorated, to name no more—seem so obvious today is largely a tribute to Palgrave's success in forming the general attitudes about poetry that most readers have held ever since.

There is nothing terribly original about most of his ideas; many of them can be traced to Johnson, the leading Romantic poets, and Ruskin's *Modern Painters.* Yet by combining and illustrating them as he did, he promoted them from the class of theories about which it is possible to argue to that of truisms which are rarely thought about at all. The most important result of his book, as I have already said, is that nearly all the longer forms of poetry came to be looked upon as less poetic than the lyric, thereby consigning whole periods in which the lyric did not flourish to oblivion. As Naomi Lewis declared some years ago in the *Listener, The Golden Treasury* put romantic pastoral England permanently at the centre of the poetic tradition, not as one subject among many but as the inescapable *locus* of the poetic muse. "At the same time," she went on, "it was to give the odd impression that what was not in its pages simply did not exist at all. . . . As a result, the classical eighteenth century was to disappear underground well into our own day."[5] Sir Alexander Grant, a colonial administrator of the 1860s, attributed to it influence of a rather different sort, writing Palgrave from Bombay that his book was "an immense comfort out here" and proposing it as a textbook for Indian students because "English poetry is to these people what Homer is to us."[6] Like the Union Jack, the Bible, and the Gatling gun, *The Golden Treasury* had quickly become an instrument of empire and a symbol of British civilization.

Its most important impact, of course, was on poets and critics nearer to home. In January 1862, three months before the young Thomas Hardy set out to seek his fortune in London, his friend Horace Moule gave him an inscribed copy of the recently published *Golden Treasury* which the aspiring poet kept, annotated, and treasured all his life. "No doubt he knew many of its poems by heart," his biographer Evelyn Hardy declares, "for he often quotes from them in his prose and has used their lines for the titles of two of his novels. More importantly still, Hardy confessed to his wife, shortly before his death, that if he ever had an ambition it was that 'some poem or poems' of his should be included 'in a good anthology like the *Golden Treasury*.'"[7] Housman too was a careful reader (and annotator), not only of the original collection but of the *Second Series* that Palgrave published in 1897.[8] And in the preface to *The Oxford Book of English Verse*, Sir Arthur Quiller-Couch paid an anthologist's tribute to the hold of his predecessor on several generations of readers:

> Few of my contemporaries can erase—or would wish to erase—the dye their minds took from the late Mr. Palgrave's *Golden Treasury*: and he who has returned to it again and again with an affection born of companionship on many journeys must remember not only what the *Golden Treasury* includes, but the moment when this or that poem appealed to him, and even how it lies on the page.[9]

Thus Palgrave's spirit underwent a kind of rebirth in the twentieth century between those famous blue covers.

Because Tennyson suggested to Palgrave the idea of producing an anthology and collaborated in making the selections, the book has often been regarded as a monument to official Victorian taste. Angus Ross's opinion is typical: "This volume, once widely used in schools and sometimes the only poetry book ever read, has many merits of selection, but has been of incalculable effect in rivetting a mid-Victorian sensibility on the English readers of poetry, for Palgrave was nothing if not backward-looking."[10] How an historical anthology could be other than backward-looking is not clear, however, and neither the choice of lyric as the model poetic form nor the standards Palgrave applied to lyrics were mid-Victorian commonplaces. Indeed, both are so far from Tennyson's own theory and practice that his presence as the book's godfather is more than a little surprising. Had Tennyson agreed to let Palgrave incorporate selections by him, it is difficult to see how he could have been represented by any poems that he would have thought major products of his art. (Tennyson's refusal to be represented at all led Palgrave to exclude living poets entirely, so that the volume concludes with the Romantics.)

In fact, the principles expressed in the preface and notes to *The Golden Treasury* and implied by Palgrave's organization and selections were not orthodox until the success of the book made them so. This is not to say, however, that Palgrave led an unwilling public (or unwilling poets) to a reversal of taste and conviction. Like so many seminal works, *The Golden Treasury* achieved quasi-scriptural status because it embodies in a clear, coherent, and compassable form ideas that were in the air. For a variety of reasons, English poetry in 1861 was ready for a lyric revival, and if Palgrave did not fully understand the reasons for such a revival, he at least managed to identify enough of the changing demands English readers would henceforth make on poetry to give his work an influence unique in the history of anthologies. We must understand these demands and their causes before we can fully appreciate what he said about the lyric and the way he organized his canon.

For reasons that are easily summarized, the Romantic and early-Victorian conception of poetry as prophecy was already well past its prime in 1861. The failure of Wordsworth's and Shelley's successors to carry out their mentors' program of a new revelation to supersede that of churches, together with the ever-stronger claims of science to be the only source of reliable information about the universe and its operations, made both poets and readers feel that the times were unpromising for the delivery of new systems of thought in verse. Tennyson, Browning, and Arnold had all once shared the vision of the poet as prophet to his civilization, and indeed the major works of the first two, at least, were received by many readers not primarily as works for esthetic enjoyment but as revelations on the most important matters of belief and conduct. Those same long works, however, when read in a more skeptical spirit, could be seen to embody more doubt than faith, more uncertainty about belief and conduct than confident advice. The major mid-Victorian poems—*In Memoriam, Idylls of the King, The Ring and the Book, Empedocles on Etna,* and so forth—are typically long works in which a small truth is won after an enormous struggle. From the standpoint of the Victorian poet's own aims—the reestablishment of security through the discovery of saving truth—none of these poems is really successful, and Arnold was being more honest than his two leading colleagues when he declined to reprint *Empedocles* in his 1853 collection because, he felt, it represented the modern temper all too well.

We will not understand Palgrave, however, unless we grasp the importance most Victorian readers continued to attach to truth in poetry. Here again Arnold is our most illuminating guide, for while he made some of the highest claims for the truth of poetry in the two and a half decades after Darwin's *Origin of Species,* he was at the same time conscious of the danger foreseen by an earlier generation of Romantic critics, that science was displacing not only religion but poetry as the teller of the most important truths. "More and more," Arnold asserted in an often-quoted passage, "mankind will discover that we have to turn to poetry to interpret life for us, to console us, to sustain us. Without poetry our science will appear incomplete; and most of what now passes with us for religion and philosophy will be replaced by poetry."[11] As I have tried to show, this is a less confident, more defensive statement than it seems to be; but the impulse behind it to defend poetry as a guide to life should not be dismissed as merely the over-earnestness of one troubled mid-Victorian humanist. Walter Pater, half a generation younger than Arnold and Palgrave, is often identified with the Esthetic Movement and the belief in art for art's sake. Nevertheless, few of his readers are likely to have quarreled with him when, as late as 1888, he had this to say about the relations between poetry, truth, and beauty: "Truth! there can be no merit, no craft at all, without that. And further, all beauty is in the long run only *fineness* of truth, or what we call expression, the finer accommodation of speech to that vision within."[12]

But how could such an accommodation take place in an increasingly agnostic age, an age when more and more readers—Arnold, Hardy, Housman, and a little later Yeats are a few examples out of many—were finding poetry of the portentous sort less and less convincing, even as they found the successive announcements of science more and more damaging to a satisfyingly coherent view of life? What role could poetry take that science would not soon seize for its own? By the nineties the Esthetics would sever the connections between poetry and truth altogether, as Poe had done earlier, thereby putting an end to all competition between poets and scientists. The smallness of their audience and their own haughty attitudes toward the larger public suggest, however, that this solution appealed to few readers. Even a Victorian scientist might feel that the value of literature was closely related to the truth it conveyed, however forcefully he might seek to repel poets from some of the domains in which they had hitherto roamed freely. Thomas Henry Huxley, whom Yeats as a young man hated for having made incredible the Christian mythology that he wished to believe,[13] did not sound very different from Arnold or Pater when he addressed the question of what made literary studies worth pursuing:

A little song of Shakespeare or of Goethe is pure art; it is exquisitely beautiful, although its intellectual content may be nothing. . . . Nevertheless, the great mass of the literature we esteem is valued, not merely because of having artistic form, but because of its intellectual content; and the value is the higher the more precise, distinct, and true is that intellectual content. And, if you will let me for a moment speak of the very highest forms of literature, do we not regard them as highest simply because the more we know the truer they seem, and the more competent we are to appreciate beauty the more beautiful they are?[14]

Beauty and truth were not to be separated. Even the St. Paul of science and coiner of the word *agnosticism*—the doctrine that we have, and probably can have, no knowledge whatever about the transcendental matters that had been such a prominent subject in poetry—was clear about that.

But what sort of truth was left for poets to write about, and how might they best accommodate—Pater's word—that truth to poetic beauty, and both to the reduced scope that poetry would henceforth be allowed? Whatever his convictions, the honest poet could no longer ignore the ways that the world had changed since Darwin. Even a work like *In Memoriam* was no longer possible after 1859; the view of the world on which it depended, and the view of the poet, had already been exploded by events. Henceforth the truths of poetry that would wear best would be flashes of insight into experience, highly focussed clarifications of life (to anticipate Robert Frost's definition of poetry), interpretive ways of seeing that at best would communicate the knowledge of a situation to readers but could never aspire to systematic or transcendental revelation. Poetry would become more modest and more subjective than it had once been—Romantic poetry had of course been subjective without being modest—and it would largely abandon the attempt to grasp the whole of life. This would be as true of most important religious poetry (Hopkins's, for example) as it would be of poems by agnostics like Hardy and Housman. By doing these things, poetry might make that series of accommodations the times demanded; it might at the same time gain in both honesty and versatility.

Given this set of requirements, the lyric would almost inevitably become the dominant mode. The crystallization of meaning in the most powerful and compressed language has been the defining characteristic of lyric poetry in literate times. The lyric and its author are interested not in happenings—true or fictional—but in their meanings, whether intellectual or emotional (or, as is usual in real life, an inseparable complex of the two). The story itself, if there was one, is abbreviated drastically or abolished. For the lyric belongs not to literature's earliest, narrative, stage, but to the stage of analysis. Of the three kinds of poetry Aristotle had identified—epic, dramatic, and lyric—the first two had been moribund in English since the seventeenth century. Now the possibilities of lyric would be more rigorously explored than ever before.

One thing that was lacking was a collection of models to define the tradition of the English lyric. The lyric had been a genre of secondary importance throughout most of the history of English poetry. Furthermore, much lyric poetry of all periods had been, as Huxley suggested, almost devoid of intellectual content. Someone would have to explain and illustrate its possibilities for both readers and aspiring poets. He need not fully understand the context in which he was acting—catalysts seldom do. If he did a good job of providing inspiration and direction, he would acquire an influence that future generations of critics would find it equally hard to understand and to abolish.

It is clear that Palgrave's aim, however guardedly expressed, was an ambitious one: to create a standard of English poetic taste that would be generally adopted. The poems he chose would constitute the approved tradition, and he warns in his preface that the omission of any hitherto highly regarded poem through inadvertence is unlikely: he has with great care decided what fits and what goes out. Hence, as he explains in the series of little essays that he misleadingly calls notes,

> a strictly representative or historical Anthology has not been aimed at. Great Excellence, in human art as in human character, has from the beginning of things been even more uniform than Mediocrity, by virtue of the closeness of its approach to Nature:—and so far as the standard of Excellence kept in view has been attained in this volume, a comparative absence of extreme or temporary phases in style, a similarity of tone and manner, will be found throughout:—something neither modern nor ancient, but true in all ages, and like the works of Creation, perfect as on the first day. (308)

The individual talent, in other words, is very much a creature of the tradition—at least insofar as it leaves genuine monuments. Dr. Johnson in the preceding century and Mr. Eliot in the next would both have approved of this sentiment.

We have already seen Palgrave's definition of lyric poetry. The read-

er who has tried to apply similar definitions to great bodies of literature might guess that Palgrave soon found himself in difficulties, but
he admits to few problems in separating the lyrical from the nonlyrical.
Since the nonlyrical is by implication destined for the second and lower
drawers of poetry, let us look at what categories of verse he explicitly
rejects: "narrative, descriptive, and didactic poems—unless accompa-
nied by rapidity of movement, brevity, and the colouring of human
passion"; "Humourous poetry, except in the very unfrequent instances where a truly poetical tone pervades the whole"; "what is
strictly personal, occasional, and religious"; "Blank verse and the ten-
syllable couplet, with all pieces markedly dramatic" (preface). He al-
lows, however, that in some doubtful cases he has chosen to include
poems—such as Gray's "Elegy," Milton's "L'Allegro" and "Il Pense-
roso," and Wordsworth's "Ruth"—that "might be claimed with perhaps equal justice for a narrative or descriptive selection; whilst with
reference especially to Ballads and Sonnets, the Editor can only state
that he has taken his utmost pains to decide without caprice or partial-
ity." Creating a standard is a serious business, and Palgrave's judicial
tone never quavers into false modesty.

Having declared his intention of assembling the best lyric poems in
the language and explained what he means by lyric, Palgrave next
turns to the seven criteria which will define the best. Rather than attempt to prove their validity, he simply lists them, which gives the
paragraph in which they appear a misleading brevity and simplicity.
The first three are commonplaces and cannot have gotten him very far:
"That a Poem shall be worthy of the writer's genius,—that it shall
reach a perfection commensurate with its aim,—that we should re-
quire finish in proportion to brevity." It is with the fourth criterion
that we come to the crux of Palgrave's standards: "that passion, col-
our, and originality cannot atone for serious imperfections in clearness,
unity, or truth."

Poetry was to embody genuine emotion; that part of the Romantic
legacy would stand. But truth, expressed clearly and with unity, was
more important still, and without truth originality was of little value.
Palgrave made no attempt to define truth directly. Obviously it does
not mean the visions of a Blake or Poe, neither of whom is represented
in the anthology. It has to be something that can be not merely com-

municated to but shared by all perceptive readers. On the other hand, he has excluded poetry of the strictly religious sort from his canon, along with explicitly didactic works. His daughter tells us that while Wordsworth was his favorite poet—which the anthology amply bears out—he felt that "the undercurrent of 'preachiness' spoiled his poetry at times."[15] A note on Scott's brief lyric "The Pride of Youth" will help us see what Palgrave meant by truth of the sort that poetry should convey and the modest, indirect way in which the conveying might be done: "No moral is drawn, far less any conscious analysis of feeling attempted:—the pathetic meaning is left to be suggested by the mere presentment of the situation. Inexperienced critics have often named this, which may be called the Homeric manner, superficial, from its apparent simple facility: but first rate excellence in it . . . is in truth one of the least common triumphs of poetry" (321-2). Truth—which Palgrave, unlike many Victorian writers, does not capitalize—means something between the extremes of the purely personal and the cosmic. Lyric poetry is neither revelation nor a private amusement; it is the exploration of experience with a very precise telescope that is capable of endlessly enlarging small areas of life. It has the ability of showing us the truth about almost anything in life—"interpreting to us the lessons of Nature" is Palgrave's phrase—because, in the hands of a master poet, it never tries to illuminate too much at once. If it does, the medium is violated, truth obscured, and the poem spoiled.

Palgrave's fifth criterion of merit is that a few good lines do not save an otherwise indifferent poem. His sixth, which interrupts the natural progression of his thought here, is that popular esteem must be taken as a guidepost, not a compass (perhaps because the public is often swayed from true north by partial truths and half-successful poems). His last criterion of poetic merit is a restatement of the fifth in different words: "above all, that Excellence should be looked for rather in the Whole than in the Parts." The lyric poems that merit a place in the tradition are unified in form and thought, small wholes in which clarity of intellectual content and intensity of emotion work together in the interests of the reader's pleasure and improvement.

Palgrave did not think that his purposes could be best served by a purely chronological arrangement of poems, and he grouped his selections in what he felt to be "the most poetically effective order." There are four books. The first covers "the ninety years closing about 1616," the second what remained of the seventeenth century, the third the eighteenth century, and the fourth poetry written after 1800 by poets who were no longer living in 1861. (In fact the fourth book consists almost entirely of Romantic verse composed before 1830.) Palgrave alludes to them in the preface as "the Books of Shakespeare, Milton, Gray, and Wordsworth," but he does not actually give them titles. Within the books, there is no attempt at chronological order. Rather the poems are "arranged in gradations of feeling or subject. The development of the symphonies of Mozart and Beethoven has been here thought of as a model, and nothing placed without careful consideration." Few anthologists since Palgrave's time can ever have taken so hierophantic a view of their duties, or striven so ingeniously to fulfill them. Not only are those lyric poems that pass the test individually models of truth and unity; so is the whole collection of such poems when orchestrated as they ought to be by an editor who knows his vocation.

With all this apparatus of self-confident purpose, what poems did Palgrave actually include in *The Golden Treasury*? Every anthologist is accused of unforgivable choices and omissions, and rather than try to weigh the book's sins and virtues let us examine the ways in which Palgrave carried out the plan announced in his preface.

The first book contains nothing earlier than Wyatt; most of the riches of the medieval lyric remained in manuscript in 1861, and in any case Palgrave would probably have found the bulk of it either too religious or too bawdy for his purposes. The very first poem in the book, appropriately enough, is Thomas Nash's "Spring." Thirty-two of Shakespeare's sonnets and songs from his plays dominate book one; there is one poem each by Sidney, Spenser, Drayton, and Marlowe, while Drummond has seven. As in the three books that follow, the sixty-one selections are grouped thematically. For example, number XLIV, Shakespeare's song "Come away, come away, Death" (which Palgrave entitles "Dirge of Love"), is followed by "Fear no more the heat of the sun" ("Fidele"), "Full fathom five" ("A Sea Dirge"), Webster's "Call for the robin redbreast and the wren" ("A Land Dirge"), Shakespeare's Sonnet 32 ("Post Mortem"), and Sonnet 71 ("The Triumph of Death"). (If Murray Prosky is correct, Eliot's close juxtaposition of the "Sea Dirge" and "Land Dirge" in *The Waste Land* owes something to Palgrave's sequence here.[16]) In the notes, Palgrave expounds his view of the materials in book one: "There is here a wide range of style . . . yet a general uniformity of tone prevails. Few readers can fail to observe the natural sweetness of the verse, the single-hearted straightforwardness of the thoughts:—nor less, the limitation of subject to the many phases of one passion" (308). We shall see these themes developed as Palgrave discusses the succeeding periods.

Book two, he announces, "contains the close of our Early poetical style and the commencement of the Modern" (311). Milton and Dryden are the dominant figures. Like Johnson, Palgrave disapproved of the Metaphysical poets, finding their work "deformed by verbal fancies and conceits of thought"; there is no Donne, while Herbert and Crashaw are represented by one poem each. Despite what one might have expected Palgrave to regard as a disabling lack of seriousness in their work, however, the Cavalier poets are present in some strength. As a stage in the evolution of English poetry, he considers the period a mixed bag. "That the change from our early style to the modern brought with it at first a loss of nature and simplicity is undeniable: yet the far bolder and wider scope which Poetry took between 1620 and 1700, and the successful efforts then made to gain greater clearness in expression, in their results have been no slight compensation" (311). Book two contains fifty-five selections, six fewer than book one; oddly enough, it includes imitations of seventeenth-century styles by Scott and Darley, the latter's mislabelled "Anonymous."

Book three represents the eighteenth century, which Palgrave found the least satisfactory period in English poetry. It is "an age not only of spontaneous transition, but of bold experiment" (316); its styles are disconcertingly various—remember that Palgrave thought the best lyric poetry was characterized by "a comparative absence of extreme or temporary phases in style, a similarity of tone and manner"—and its tone best "explained by reference to its historical origin" in an age of bold inquiry. Pope has only one selection, a juvenile piece, in comparison with Gray's eight. Palgrave pays tribute to his poets' high intentions, but clearly he feels that their century was too confusing a time to produce much satisfactory verse; this book is the shortest of the four, with only forty-nine selections, although it covers the longest period of any.

It is when we come to the fourth book that we find Palgrave at his most enthusiastic. Despite the fact that it covers, in effect, only thirty years, book four contains one hundred twenty-three poems, making it more than twice as long as book one. The nineteenth century is the culmination of the historical tendencies Palgrave had identified in the poetry of earlier centuries; its writers therefore have opportunities denied to their predecessors. Wordsworth is overwhelmingly the major figure here, with forty-one selections, and the reader of *The Golden Treasury* might never suspect that he had written anything longer than the "Intimations Ode," which is the penultimate selection in the volume. Shelley follows, with Keats, Scott, and Campbell close behind. Coleridge is represented by only two selections, both minor. On the Romantics as a whole, Palgrave has this to say:

> These Poets, with others, carried to further perfection the later tendencies of the century preceding, in simplicity of narrative, reverence for human Passion and Character in every sphere, and impassioned love of Nature: . . . whilst maintaining on the whole the advances in art made since the Restoration, they renewed the half-forgotten melody and depth of tone which marked the best Elizabethan writers: . . . lastly, to what was thus inherited they added a richness in language and a variety in metre, a force and fire in narrative, a tenderness and bloom in feeling, an insight into the finer passages of the Soul and the inner meanings of the landscape, a larger and wise Humanity,— hitherto hardly attained, and perhaps unattainable even by predecessors of not inferior individual genius. (320)

What Palgrave's two hundred eighty-eight selections and the notes that elucidate them add up to, then, is a thoroughly evolutionary view of poetry. Because the poetry of each period is "a more or less unconscious mirror of the genius of the age" (317), each individual poet's opportunities are largely determined—and circumscribed—by the times in which he lives. The pattern of development that Palgrave found in English poetry may be summarized as follows: the Elizabethans, at the beginning of the tradition, had the naturalness of melody and depth of tone that befitted a relatively unsophisticated age; their lyric lacked scope, however, and was on the whole minor for that reason. In the seventeenth century lyric poets learned how to deal with a much greater variety of subjects. At first, this expansion of range carried with it a loss of naturalness, but with Dryden clarity—the most important stylistic virtue for poetry as a bearer of truth—returned. The eighteenth century to some extent repeated the pattern of the seventeenth, but the growth of knowledge and inquiry was so rapid that not until the Romantics came on the scene was poetry able to assimilate it. The nineteenth-century poet, however, is in a position to unite all the discoveries of previous centuries: the depth and naturalness of the Elizabethans, the scope and clarity of the seventeenth century, and the sense of continual new discovery that characterized the eighteenth.[17]

Thus the rise of science and the increase in positive knowledge need not be a disadvantage to the nineteenth-century poet at all, at least not to the lyric poet. Poetry could retain its place in the scientific age so long as it continued the tradition as codified and did not become too eccentric in form or meaning. The curve of poetry over the last three hundred years led upwards, not (as Macaulay, Peacock, and so many other critics had been saying) to its extinction in a world that was intellectually outgrowing it. More excellent poems had been written in the first three decades of the nineteenth century than in any previous century, and only the modesty of the Poet-Laureate prevented his young admirer from carrying the story down to the present. A careful examination of the history of English poetry could only inspire optimistic conclusions about its future. The opportunities ahead would be obvious to any aspiring poet into whose hands the book fell.

First published in July 1861, *The Golden Treasury* was reprinted three times before the end of the year. Its continued success led Palgrave to produce several enlarged versions, then a second edition in 1891 that brought the total number of poems to three hundred thirty-nine. (The additions came mainly in book one, as a result of new scholarly works that increased Palgrave's knowledge of Elizabethan poetry.) Meanwhile, in 1875, he published a *Children's Treasury of Lyric Poetry* designed shrewdly both for children's "own possession and study, not less than for use as a class-book in the teacher's hand."[18] With the proviso that the poems in it should all be morally and intellectually suitable for readers between the ages of nine and sixteen, the collection represents essentially the same tastes and intentions as *The Golden Treasury* and has been frequently reprinted. Wordsworth again had the largest number of selections, followed by Shakespeare and Shelley; this time Blake was represented. By the time Palgrave was elected Professor of Poetry at Oxford, in 1885, Macmillan's Golden Treasury Series incorporated not only his anthologies but his editions of lyrics by Keats, Herrick, Shakespeare, and Tennyson, as well as a plethora of anthologies and editions by other people.

In 1897, the year of his death, Palgrave published *The Golden Treasury: Second Series* to bring his original collection up to date. The volume never acquired the popularity or influence of the original anthology, perhaps because Palgrave felt an unwonted uncertainty about what to include, but he took the occasion in its preface to survey the course of the lyric revival as it had progressed since his original terminus. In it he found grounds for both satisfaction (one might almost say self-satisfaction) and disapproval: "A decided preference for lyrical poetry,—to which in all ages the perplexed or overburdened heart has fled for relief and confession,—has shown itself for sixty years or more; an impulse traceable in large measure to the increasingly *subjective* temper of the age, and indeed already in different phases foreshown by Shelley and by Wordsworth."[19] Whether he approved of the temper of the age he did not indicate, but he went on acutely to consider the changes it had brought about in lyric poetry. The lyric, having nearly driven its competitors from the field, was beginning to swallow them, a consequence of triumph unforeseen in 1861:

> From this preference (whilst the national or commemorative Ode has become rare), followed also a vast extension in length of our lyrics: their work is apt to be less concentrated than that of their predecessors, classical or English: whilst, concurrently, they have at the same time often taken a dramatic character, rarely to be found before.

The monologues of Browning were now part of the tradition. Both he and Tennyson were dead. *A Shropshire Lad* had recently been published. "Prufrock" was only fifteen years in the future.

Whether Palgrave at the end of his life felt himself in the position of a successful revolutionary whose successors had betrayed his intentions he does not tell us, but there can be no doubt about his success. As we have seen, *The Golden Treasury* continued to be read as something approaching holy writ by poets and scholars long after his death. His effect on common readers of poetry, though less easily documented, has almost certainly been greater. Indeed, Palgrave did more than anyone else to create late-Victorian poetic taste and assumptions about poetry—a taste and set of assumptions which, so far as nonacademic readers go, have probably not changed very much in the eight decades since he left the scene. *The Golden Treasury* has never gone out of print and exists today in a variety of updated editions. Updating it is a relatively easy task because the popular poets of the twentieth century—Kipling, Housman, Bridges, Masefield, Frost, and so on—fit so well into the tradition that Palgrave defined. Even much of Yeats and Eliot can be incorporated without seeming altogether out of place.

A new generation of rebels, of course, found Palgrave and the assumptions he represented barring the path into the modern era. As one critic complained thirty years ago:

> By excluding or only slightly representing more knotty and "difficult" poets like Donne and his successors; by at first passing over Blake, so that he appears only in the later copyright editions; most of all by emphasizing nature poetry, especially the Wordsworthian kind, Palgrave has unintentionally directed taste away from the less sweet but tougher kind of poetry that has influenced poets in our own day. And further, because he confined his choice to lyrical poetry . . . many readers for whom his collection has been the key to poetry have come to think of the lyric as the only poetry *par excellence*. [20]

One reason that the nonacademic audience for poetry is so small today is undoubtedly the enormous gap in taste between most of those who write poetry (the heirs of modernism) and most ordinary readers (the heirs of Palgrave). Among poets, critics, and professional students of literature in the last half-century, Palgrave's reputation has paid the price of this split, for his lasting influence on taste has been a potent source of frustration to the modernist movement and its supporters. The aged Yeats compared Ezra Pound, the literary revolutionary, to Maud Gonne, the revolutionary nationalist, for the amusement of a correspondent. "Ezra has most of Maud Gonne's opinions. . . . The chief difference is that he hates Palgrave's *Golden Treasury,* as she hates the Irish Free State Government, and thinks even worse of its editor than she does of President Cosgrave."[21]

FIVE

New Bottles

To make a start,
out of particulars
and make them general, rolling
up the sum, by defective means—
Sniffing the trees,
just another dog
among a lot of dogs. What
else is there? And to do?
The rest have run out—
after the rabbits.
Only the lame stands—on
three legs.

William Carlos Williams, *Paterson*

"It appears likely that poets in our civilization, as it exists at present, must be *difficult*," T.S. Eliot wrote in 1921. The poet's task, he went on, is to render that civilization in all its "variety and complexity"; the results will inevitably be as various and complex as the civilization. "The poet must become more and more comprehensive, more allusive, more indirect."[1] (*The Waste Land* would be published a year later.) It has often been suggested that at the moment when the majority of serious poets began (not entirely through Eliot's influence) to write according to this dictum, serious poetry in England and America began rapidly to lose what was left of its audience.

That is to say, when poets came to regard as their chief function the reflection in all its rapidly changing details of actual contemporary life—whether through symbols or direct description, and whether the emphasis was on confession or the external world—poetry became paradoxically more difficult to read, and the familiar series of phenomena began: the decline in the number of original books of poetry published from year to year, the disappearance of poetry as a major literary form, the virtual extinction of the self-supporting poet. Poetry, as we have seen, was already gravely weakened as a cultural force before any of the leading modernists were born. Their response to the crisis they inherited was to make drastic changes in their art so that it might, as Eliot advised, mirror the world as it was and thereby regain at least the moral basis for a revival of influence. In doing so, they repudiated and even ridiculed their immediate predecessors' ideals and practices, most obviously in the area of poetic form, which henceforth was to be radically variable so as better to reflect the inner and outer realities that modernist poetry was to take as its subjects. It is curious that poets should have taken upon themselves many of the burdens of realism (a term that all the leading modernists would have scorned), in language and content, at almost precisely the time when the traditionally realistic novel was seeking other, often more traditionally poetic modes of expression. It is even more ironic that in the process of becoming less narrowly selective in its subjects and adopting free verse and a closer approximation of everyday language as its most conspicuous formal characteristics, poetry should have become less rather than more accessible to the common reader.

Toward the end of his life, William Carlos Williams had this to say about his poetic purposes: "I've always wanted to fit poetry into the life around us. . . . I abandoned the rare world of H.D. and Ezra Pound. Poetry should be brought into the world where we live and not be so recondite, so removed from the people. . . . This seemed to me to be what a poem was for, to speak for us in a language we can understand." To another interviewer at about the same time, the author of *Paterson* sounded a rather different bugle: "I acknowledge that the difficulty of a poet's writing is a barrier to the public. Definitely. But I say he is forced to it in the modern world—to reflect the complexity of his thinking. . . . When I see a poet who's perfectly clear, I have to laugh. He isn't SAYING anything."[2] Something, clearly, had gone wrong, something that went to the roots of the modernist enterprise.

Poetic modernism might seem to defeat generalization, so diverse have been its sources, movements, and aims. It is hardly surprising that modernism's chief critical offspring, the New Criticism, largely denied the value of literary history and demanded exclusive attention to the work on the page. Nevertheless, the leading modernists—Pound, Eliot, Williams, Stevens, Auden—and their followers shared, or were shared by, certain assumptions about poetry that were inherent in their poetic practices. Modernism in literature was tacitly predicated on the hypothesis that human experience in the twentieth century is radically discontinuous with that of the past and can be rendered only through radically new artistic structures. This discontinuity might look different from different angles; it might mean (as in the early left-wing Auden or the populist Williams) that the twentieth century offers unprecedented opportunities for the common man and his poetic celebrators, or on the contrary it might mean (as to Eliot and the later Auden) that our age is uniquely unfortunate in having lost a spiritual, intellectual, and artistic unity possessed by all centuries before the nineteenth. It might even be possible for some poets to believe both these things at the same time. In any case, the employment of both radical and reactionary poetic strategies followed: on the one hand, the use of free verse, fragmentation of syntax, deliberately unpoetic diction, subjects which had rarely or never appeared in poetry before; on the other, the increasing cultivation of myth as a structure for organizing experience (traditional poetic organization having been largely abandoned), nostalgic references to medieval religion, and quotations from classical or Renaissance literature on a grand scale.

As its name implies, modernism can be understood only as a reaction against what had gone before, however ambiguously defined the rejected past might be. Modernism in poetry, as in architecture, included the premise that form follows function; the set forms of traditional English poetry were to be abandoned because they were at best imperfectly adapted to any particular poetic content. Modernist poems would determine their own forms organically. Thus they would in theory be much more varied than traditional poems, and the variety would be a healthy one. Life, after all, does not come neatly packaged in (say) fourteen-line units. To reflect experience—contemporary or otherwise—most faithfully, poems should get below our normal presuppositions about both life and poetry. That such procedures would disturb many readers whose assumptions about life were conventional and whose poetic expectations were based on Palgrave and similar critics was obvious from the start, but the risk of alienating potential readers was accepted. Our ordinary way of reading poetry represents "the mind in its least active state"; modernist poets should demand more.

Although modernist practice was usually seen as a reaction to Victorian poetry, it was, at least in theory, independent of any particular era; it represented a set of beliefs about poetry that held true for all time, a return to ideals that were valid in all times and places even if, as a matter of historical fact, they had rarely or never been fully put into practice. In their *Survey of Modernist Poetry* (1927), still the best book on the subject, Laura Riding and Robert Graves described an ideal modernism which, they made clear, was often far from the practice of the poets they were surveying:

> *Modernist,* indeed, should describe a quality in poetry which has nothing to do with the date or with responding to civilization. Poetry to which *modernist* in this sense could be fully applied would derive its excellence neither from its reacting against civilization, by satiric or actual primitivism; nor from its proved ability to keep up with or keep ahead of civilization. It would not, however, ignore its contemporaneous universe, for the reason that it would not be stupid and that it would have a sense of humour—the most intelligent attitude toward history is not to take one's own date too seriously. There would occur evidences of time in such poetry; but always its modernism would lie in its independence, in its relying on none of the traditional devices of poetry-making in the past nor on any of the artificial effects to be got by using the atmosphere of contemporary life and knowledge to startle or to give reality.[3]

That this independence was rarely to be found in actual modernist poetry was a fact of which Riding and Graves were extremely critical. The ideal was far from being realized, for it was much easier to be modern in the superficial sense of merely up-to-date than to acquire the detachment and ease that are being recommended here. Indeed, the fatal defect in actual modernism was its compulsive propensity to depict contemporary civilization, whether favorably or satirically, and to bemuse itself with the merely new.

Despite the contradictions and instabilities at its center, in some ways the modernist impulse was well adapted to a more truthful poetry than the Victorians had often produced. As Riding and Graves astutely noted:

> When the prestige of any organization is curtailed—the army or navy for example—a greater internal discipline, morality and study of tactics results, a greater sophistication and up-to-dateness. In poetry this discipline means the avoidance of all the wrongly-conceived habits and tactics of the past: poetry becomes so sophisticated that it seems to know at last how it should be written and written at the very moment. (262-63)

But by the very nature of this sophistication, the dangers of mere eccentricity (which would be difficult to detect in the absence of traditional standards) and contempt for the reader were always present. Poetic modernism at its best involved using the connotative and allusive powers of words and phrases (not always quoted) to their maximum, but in a more controlled and economical way than Romantic or Victorian poetry. Thus it joined some of the most important features of classicism and romanticism. Unfortunately, most of its practitioners were unable or unwilling to walk such a fine line and soon fell off, either into an excess of obscure suggestiveness or into a neoclassical irony so dry as to seem embalmed. Pound and Eliot at their best, but only at their best, managed to avoid both: hence the emotional lucidity of, for example, "Marina" and the last sections of *Canto 81*.

Whether—and if so how—such poetry should convey significant ideas or was simply an object to be admired became one of the most vexed questions in twentieth-century criticism, largely because Eliot in his enormously influential critical writings often denounced the view that poetry ought to have intellectual content. Poe and his successors, of whom in this sense Eliot was one, saw the danger of identifying poetry with messages: when the messages ceased to please or seem important, the reader would go elsewhere for better ones. Furthermore, the adequacy of the ideas themselves becomes a standard by which to judge the poem—an illegitimate standard, Eliot and his critical successors felt, for a work of art should be judged solely by artistic criteria, which were assumed to exclude an evaluation of content. For this and other reasons, they gave currency to the notion of the autonomous poem, whose relations with the outside world are as irrelevant as those of a string quartet. Insofar as it was truly poetic, the poem had no ideas and therefore could not be paraphrased; its life was an entirely independent one. Since ideas are always about something outside the poem itself, they naturally limit its autonomy. As a way of defending poetry, this conception had a certain attractiveness, for the unparaphrasable poem's function and value could not, by definition, be assumed by any other medium. It was also useful protection against the misguided demands of the "plain reader," who, as Riding and Graves put it, "while he does not object to the poetic state of mind in the poet, has a fear of cultivating it himself. This is why he prefers the prose summary to the poem and to see the poem, as it began in the poet's mind, as a genial prose idea free of those terrors which the poet is supposed to keep to himself or carefully disguise" (149-50). Here as in so many other ways, art often imitated criticism. "I should say," the mature Eliot pronounced, "that in one's prose reflexions one may be legitimately occupied with ideas, whereas in the writing of verse one can only deal with actuality."[4]

Like the objective correlative and the notion of impersonality, this statement is a step toward making poetry autonomous, and therefore once more possessed of a unique role. But the assumption that a meaningful distinction can be made between words-about-actuality and words-expressing-ideas is as odd as the limitation Eliot here seeks to impose on poetry. And the tactic involved—surrendering the very field on which the battle was being waged, by asserting that poetry had never properly possessed the sorts of intellectual content that had always been assumed for it—does not seem altogether promising. That literature in this respect was fundamentally different from such arts as music, painting, and sculpture because words, unlike tones, colors, and marble, always convey intellectual content was a notion that many twentieth-century critics resisted. Where ideas were obviously present, it became the critical fashion to refer them back to a "persona" who existed solely within the poem—whether the poem was ostensibly dramatic or not—and thereby evade the whole issue of the poem's intellectual relations with the outside world, or with its now impersonalized author. (Another, possibly more fruitful, kind of impersonality—in which the poem focused the reader's attention on its subject and minimized his awareness of its own style and structure—has rarely been advocated in the twentieth century.) As poetry became more distinct from other activities and kinds of writing, so criticism made its reading a more specialized, even professional task, divorced from the search for meaning that had been the main source of its interest for nonspecialists.

What is most odd about the ideal of the autonomous poem, however, is its remoteness from the mature practice of the leading modernist poets. If we ignore for the moment almost everything that modernist poets and critics have said about the autonomy of the work, early-twentieth-century poetry looks very different: distinct from that of the past in technique, obviously, but otherwise very much what one might have expected to find half a century after Arnold and Hopkins. In its major concerns—the paralyzing self-consciousness of the modern intellectual, the rejection of urban industrial society, the search for spiritual commitment—the mature poetry of Pound and Eliot follows directly from the Victorian mainstream. (Continuity with the recent past is even more obvious in the case of Yeats, who is most accurately seen not as a modernist but as a supremely talented late-nineteenth-century lyricist who was influenced in mid-career by some features of modernism.) The conspicuousness of technical innovation in Pound and Eliot, coupled with the critical insistence that poems are "objects" whose structure and content are inseparable, has prevented most readers from grasping these continuities. The greater revolution was in criticism, not in poetry.

In a recent book, M.L. Rosenthal describes the practices of Yeats, Pound, and Eliot. "Their main artistic contribution is the modulation toward a poetry of open process, largely presentative, which tends toward a balancing of volatile emotional states."[5] In achieving this breakthrough to a new kind of poetry, all three poets used "the past"—whether in the form of Odyssean myth, Irish rebellion, or Elizabethan grandeur—as a frequent substitute for "conventional narrative or logical structure." The past as they conceived it, Rosenthal believes, was "a living pressure and presence, a source of strength rather than anxiety." Its use was another step toward the autonomous poem. A reader less obsessed with technique than most twentieth-century poets and critics have been, however, might argue that by pretending the past was present, all three poets (though least of all Eliot) patronized and misused it as a substitute for "logical structure," mining it simply for images or rationalizations to represent their own emotional states. Yeats's and Pound's views of the past were notoriously inaccurate and had something to do with the foolish political views that both men embodied in their poetry. It was hardly a poetic "strength" for Pound, in any but the most trivial sense, to contemplate as present a mythical past in which artists walked with tyrants and there was no *usura*.

Rosenthal, a representative modernist critic, criticizes all three poets repeatedly for their "tendentiousness," a point which gives the game away. His criticism is directed not so much at the shallowness or maliciousness of particular ideas as at the advocacy of any ideas at all in poetry. In this view he is critically orthodox—and blind to much of what is actually going on in many of the poems he discusses. Such an emphasis leads him to find the last three sections of "Little Gidding" unsatisfactory because they are "heavily didactic." While the second (Dantean) section of the same poem has an "ultimate emotional force" that makes it one of the high points of Eliot's art, the rest of the work is dominated by a "heavy dose of sheer prosiness" that is only occasionally redeemed by good lines (62-64). Whether Eliot at the last moment of his poetic career chose the best way of expressing what he wanted to say is of course open to debate, but to complain that the poem suffers *because* he was trying to say something is a perverseness peculiar to twentieth-century criticism. As Eliot himself granted on another occasion: "to be a 'pure artist' is by no means incompatible with having 'an axe to grind'. Virgil and Dante had plenty of axes on the grindstone; Dickens and George Eliot are often at their best when they are grinding axes; and Flaubert is no exception. Unless there was grinding of axes, there would be very little to write about."[6]

Despite the sometime protestations of Eliot and the other leading modernists, didacticism—the advocacy of political, social, and religious ideas—may in fact be one of the most important features of their mature poetry. The development of the three poets mentioned above is not toward the poem-as-object, but away from it, toward the poem as didactic myth. The New Criticism has been a misleading guide to the poems of the leading modernists, who soon outgrew the autonomous phase of their development as poets. Who, after all, would plow his way through *The Waste Land* if it were really, as Eliot maintained and Rosenthal approvingly quotes, "only the relief of a personal and wholly insignificant grouse against life" rather than an intellectually formidable diagnosis and prescription for a whole civilization? How many readers of Yeats's later historical and political poems would trade their "tendentiousness," however misguided it sometimes is, for the self-conscious artiness of the early Yeats?

Three years or so before his death, a father of twentieth-century poetry, Walt Whitman, directed this legacy to his successors:

> Whatever may have been the case in years gone by, the true use for the imaginative faculty of modern times is to give ultimate vivification to facts, to science, and to common lives, endowing them with the glows and glories and final illustriousness which belong to every real thing, and to real things only. Without that ultimate vivification—which the poet or other artist alone can give—reality would seem incomplete, and science, democracy, and life itself, finally in vain. [7]

To treat this eloquent plea merely as a variant of Arnold's "soft argument" for poetic truth would be to ignore its visionary quality. Life in the twentieth century, carrying further the developments of the nineteenth, was going to be different from the past in quality as well as in detail; by completing it in his own vision, as opposed to simply describing it, the poet might render indispensable service to his readers and join the present to the past in the communion of all "real things." That Whitman's view of poetry as expressed here has not been a major force in actual twentieth-century poetry is not surprising. The visionary tradition has always been a distinguished but a subordinate one and remains so in the works of Allen Ginsberg, Denise Levertov, Robert Duncan, and other writers to whom in many respects the twentieth century looks very much as the seventeenth looked to Thomas Traherne. To such poets, the outer world is not essentially distinct from the inner—which is not to say that they lack the ability to distinguish between the two, but rather that they do not follow the modern habit of subordinating the inner to the outer which has come to be defined as the essence of sanity.

In some periods, those in which vision and allegory flourish, poets try to make the inner world external and objective; in others, they see the outer world as inner and subjective. The boundary between the inner and outer is often not very clear or important in poetry, which is one major reason that the typical modern mind finds poetry so unsettling. For the "modern" view of the world derived from popularizations of science is based on a rigid separation of the two, and sees the inner as being of dependent and secondary importance. Indeed, the inner world is generally thought worthy of extended consideration only if it can be *reduced* to the outer, as in the theoretically objective and impersonal terms of psychology. The experience of the first person can be "studied" and validated only if put in abstract third-person terms, even though no one has ever experienced anything except privately, subjectively, personally.

Literary and psychological cliché to the contrary, the typical modern reader in England and America has been conditioned to an extreme degree of extroversion. Seldom in any previous period have the dictates of the inner world—whether defined psychologically, morally, spiritually, or poetically—been so patronized or mistrusted. As Whitman's declaration implies, all experience is both inner and outer at the same time: life is simultaneously both subjective and objective. To forget this basic fact about experience is to fall into one of two opposite, but similar, kinds of alienation, each of which has led to a distinct kind of modern poem. If more poets after Whitman had been able to avoid an exaggerated, one-sided emphasis on either the subjective or the objective side of their art, twentieth-century poetry might have done better in overcoming its difficulties and living up to its opportunities.

Instead, the twentieth-century mind, poetic or otherwise, has tended either to seek refuge from chaos in successive forms of quasi-scientific objectivity, or to retreat from an all-too-real world into the labyrinths of the self. The second tendency, when pursued by poets, has led not so much to genuinely visionary poetry—which requires a rare kind of talent—as to a confessional poetry which, in its indulgence of the emotions, quickly became as rigidly conventional in form and in the sins which it confessed as any previous genre of poetry had ever been. The first, the doctrine of objectivity, led both to the writing of poetry about objects (Pound: "direct treatment of the 'thing'"; Williams: "No ideas but in things") and to a revival of the conception of the poem as itself an object, curiously and carefully wrought, beautiful in the same way that statues (the subjects of several early Pound poems) are beautiful. Oddly, at the same time as this "Imagist" notion of poetry gained its brief ascendancy, most of the distinctively poetic ways of creating beauty were abandoned or greatly curtailed—special poetic language, meter, rhyme. What resulted, apart from a lasting tendency in criticism, was a small number of jewel-like poems that most commonly led the reader, when they were pointed out to him, to admire their color, glint, and carefully hewn facets, and then walk on to another part of the museum. The poetry of objects—whether the object was the topic or the poem itself—was simply too limited in interest, its meanings too quickly exhausted, its creation too artificial. As I have already pointed out, the leading modernists soon abandoned it, though it has been frequently revived.

Keats had said, a century before the triumph of modernism, that poetry must fall like leaves from the tree, and had written of a nightingale that sang unheard (except by the mortal poet) for age after age. Yeats towards the end of that century wrote in "Adam's Curse" of how "A line will take us hours maybe; / Yet if it does not seem a moment's thought, / Our stitching and unstitching has been naught" and later created a mechanical nightingale made of gold who sang to sleepy emperors in a dying civilization. Nothing comes as easily to the modern poet as it did even in Keats's time, and the myths that Yeats settled upon to convey his truths were laboriously wrought artificial creations, often as difficult in the reading as in the writing. Yet it may be that Yeats and Eliot between them had settled upon a method that would, in the latter's words, be a step towards "making the modern world possible for art."[8] For myth, whether archaic or newly created, had the merit of dissolving the categories of the mind; it was a sort of collective vision, neither wholly inner nor wholly outer but merging the two in a realm that bound past and present, the material and the spiritual. With the help of myth and mythologized history Yeats had accomplished the stupendous feat of making backwater Ireland stand for the twentieth-century world; with the help of other myths (like Yeats's, derived from the books of scholars) Eliot had powerfully unified his vision of a modern civilization in fragments. Others would imitate these feats in lands even less promising for poetry.

The mythic method raised in acute form the problem of sincerity: did the artist really believe what he was saying, or expect his audience to believe it? Was the researched myth merely a substitute for genuine vision? The answer would vary with the poet. The problem of obscurity would also arise, as in the instances mentioned, when the myths that the poet used to organize his material were no longer the common knowledge of his audience. Indeed, he might find himself footnoting his poem with learned references, thereby defeating some of the purposes for which he had turned to myth in the first place. For while myth might unite form, feeling, and idea, and thereby solve some of the problems the twentieth-century poet felt in dealing with his materials, it frequently aggravated the already difficult problem of communicating with an actual twentieth-century audience, who neither knew much about myths nor were likely to believe that anything of importance could be better stated figuratively than directly.

Nevertheless, the inspiration of Yeats and Eliot (and of the Pound who had put Odysseus at the centre of his *Cantos*) led many later poets and critics to consider a mythology—whether believed and shared or not—to be indispensable in the creation of major poetry. Somehow the myth would break down walls that modern civilization and the intellect had created. Some critics hoped it might even lead to a new primitivism in which the poet-shaman would once again be a dominant figure. Whitman's declaration of purpose was accordingly modified by Cyril Connolly, who avowed in the 1950s: "Today the function of the artist is to bring imagination to science and science to imagination, where they meet, in the myth."[9] The factual representation of the word and its transformation through the unifying imagination might be merged into a single act of prophecy. Both the unity of western civilization and the primacy of the poet would be restored—if only people would listen.

It became evident very early, however, that the fascination with eccentricity and the merely new was inherent in modernism and could not be overcome except by a *rapprochement* with the poetic past that few modernists were able to make. (That Eliot succeeded in making it was an indispensable condition of his later poetry.) As Riding and Graves discerningly admonished in 1927:

> The most serious flaw in poetic modernism has been its attachment to originality. The modernist poet has not been able to forsake originality however directly it might contradict the classical idea of discipline; and the effect of discipline has therefore only been to make originality more original. As originality increased and as modernist poetry consequently became more and more romantic, the contradiction between it and modernist criticism was intensified. Criticism became more dogmatic and unreal, poetry more eccentric and chaotic.[10]

This widening gap we have already seen. Modernism produced a number of great works in its first generation—some of Pound's translations, "Homage to Sextus Propertius," "Hugh Selwyn Mauberley"; Eliot's "Prufrock" and *The Waste Land*; some of the early works of Stevens and Williams—and then disintegrated as a coherent set of attitudes. What had looked like a major new movement in poetry exhausted itself within a decade or two and could not be revived. For it depended, as a distinct tendency, on the shock value of the really new; it involved playing the real or mythical past against the present in a contrast that could be worked effectively only until people got used to it. Its very essence was to be revolutionary. As soon as it became orthodox—which happened very quickly—it ceased to be itself, and its leaders had only two choices if they wished to go on writing: to become figures in a new establishment (like Eliot), or to become ever more outrageous poetically and socially in a vain effort to regain the initiative of the first insurrectionary decade (like Pound). The only remaining alternative was to cease writing altogether (like Laura Riding) because the relations between truth and poetic practice had become so confused.

Modernism's chief legacy to the present is the overvaluing of the new, which has led to increasingly frantic changes in style as the heirs of the first generation split into smaller and smaller factions, each desperately trying to recapture the atmosphere of 1912. As a dominant mode, modernism is self-contradictory; hence the bewildering fragmentation of English and American poetry in the last sixty years, its increasing specialization and remoteness from other activities, its obsession with theory and technique. The excesses of modernism must bear much of the blame for aggravating the difficulties in which poetry found itself at the beginning of the twentieth century. Whatever isolated masterpieces they wrote, the leading modernists not only did not solve the question of poetry's role in a civilization dominated by science and technological industrialism, they made matters worse by imitating the latter in turning out ever-new poetic models.

Torn by contradictions—dislike of the modern world versus a compulsion to be up-to-date; rejection of the recent past versus a nostalgia for the remote that led them to distort both almost out of recognition; artistic snobbery versus the desire for community—they were victims of twentieth-century civilization in much the same way that Matthew Arnold felt himself a victim of the nineteenth. In any case, with the exception of Eliot's *Four Quartets,* few of their later works lived up to the promise of the first decade. Pound's *Cantos,* Williams's *Paterson,* H.D.'s *The Walls Do Not Fall*—the poems became longer and crankier, more pottily prophetic, less and less readable, as if their authors were trying to leap backwards over the lyric revival and recreate mid-Victorian portentousness. Eliot saw the fatal contrast between Riding and Graves's ideal modernism and the real thing earlier than most; his complaint of 1935 might apply to readers and writers then and now:

> For the reader of contemporary literature is not, like the reader of the established great literature of all time, exposing himself to the influence of divers and contradictory personalities; he is exposing himself to a mass movement of writers who, each of them, think that they have something individually to offer, but are really all working together in the same direction. . . . There never was a time so completely parochial, so shut off from the past.[11]

SIX

Grecian Thoughts in
the Home Fields

Equipped with Grecian thoughts, how could I live
Among my father's folk? My father's house
Was narrow, and his fields were nauseous.

John Crowe Ransom, "The School" (1919)

Poetic modernism was largely the creation of expatriates living in cosmopolitan cities, a fact that has had much to do with the character and concerns of twentieth-century verse. Among other things, modernism was a reaction to directions poetry had taken in the recent past and an attempt to reassert its authority (however defined) in an age the leading modernists saw as rootless, cut off from both the past and any sense of significant place. The resurrection of forgotten myths was a way of dealing with this rootlessness. Had the modernist poets shared with their public a common devotion to more landmarks—geographical, religious, and historical—their reliance on dead traditions would undoubtedly have been less. The desperate concern of so many twentieth-century poets with tradition is an indication of its absence, at least in any forms that are easily available either to the poet or to his audience. If at the beginning of the twentieth century there had existed a unified body of beliefs, memories, and loyalties that bound poet and public together in a genuine community, the modernist revolution could hardly have taken place at all. The absence of such cultural cohesion tempted if it did not actually force poets in eccentric directions, and became itself a major subject of modernist poetry.

In a few outlying regions, of course, a common body of beliefs, symbols, and associations did survive. For the most part these were backward areas where neither science nor industrialism had yet gone very far in breaking down the traditional way of life. Far from London or New York, such places did not seem very attractive to most poets, at least to poets who were not natives. Even poets born in such a region might well reject its provinciality, head for more cosmopolitan surroundings, and divest themselves of all regional taint. The urbanity and aloofness of so many leading modernists certainly encouraged such a course of action. Who could imagine the mature Eliot in St. Louis, or Pound in Idaho?

The alternative, however—to stay at home, or return home, and try to make poetry out of one's own regional materials—offered the advantages of the living tradition whose absence in the larger world Eliot and Pound so often bewailed. The use of local traditions might be fraught with problems, particularly if the poet's education had partly or wholly alienated him from regional superstitions. Nevertheless, the rewards of success could be great, as Yeats had demonstrated in Ireland: not only the creation of major poetry out of living materials, but also an end (at least in some degree) to the alienation that was the fate of the poet in most of the modern English-speaking world. A poet might serve the needs of his region by celebrating it in a way that was the opposite of naive or provincial; he might be rewarded by a rare sense of belonging, an enviable solidarity with the community around him. More important for poetry, he might also solve some of the problems of writing effective poems in the twentieth century.

The American South about 1920 was precisely the sort of region for such an experiment. Agricultural, devoted to its own ample past, inward-looking, it exerted a powerful attraction and an almost equally powerful repulsion on those of its children whose education and experience gave them some detachment in seeing it and some choice in the matter of whether to live there or elsewhere. Its literary possibilities had long been recognized, though not yet very effectively exploited. Clearly, the problems of exploiting them in poetry would be different from the problems that poets faced in more urbane surroundings. Despite the extraordinary poetic talent and sophistication that soon began to flourish in the South, some of the most serious of those problems have never been solved. The experiment of highly educated poets deliberately immersing themselves in the cultural symbols of a backward province, however, gave rise to what might be called (paraphrasing Stalin) "modernism in one country." The triumphs and failures of Southern regionalism—the self-conscious poetic cultivation of native soil—illuminate some shadowy aspects of twentieth-century poetry. One of these is its real or potential relation to living mythology, as opposed to myths that are safely dead. Another is its always problematic links with prose fiction.

Edmund Wilson, reviewing *Fugitives: An Anthology of Verse* for the *New Republic* (7 March 1928), had some shrewd and favorable things to say about the future of Southern literature. The Fugitive poets themselves he hailed as "one of the many recent manifestations of the new awakening of creative activity in the South." Furthermore the South itself, in Wilson's view, had special literary advantages and opportunities not shared by any other region of the country, not even (surprisingly) by New England:

> By reason of its very leisure, its detachment from the industrial world and its strong local tradition, the South at present enjoys unique advantages for the cultivation of literature; and it is not impossible to imagine its playing, in respect to the great cities of the North and the West, a role similar in some respects to that which eighteenth-century Ireland has played in respect to modern London. It is perhaps the only section of the country where the educated classes possess at once enough cultivation, existences sufficiently unhurried and an intimate enough share in the life of their communities to produce intellectual work of real richness and depth.

The relations of "intellectual work" to creative literature are an endlessly debatable question, but half a century after the Fugitive *Anthology* no one, not even H.L. Mencken if he were still alive, would deny that Wilson's prophecy has been fulfilled to a spectacular degree. In 1928 Faulkner and Thomas Wolfe were at the beginning of their careers and Eudora Welty a student; Robert Penn Warren, whose poems in the *Anthology* Wilson singled out for special praise, was a youth of twenty-three; William Styron, Walker Percy, Flannery O'Connor, and James Dickey were children, and Reynolds Price had yet to be born. In 1929, the year after Wilson's review, both *The Sound and the Fury* and *Look Homeward, Angel* were published. In 1930 came *Flowering Judas* and *I'll Take My Stand*. The "literary renaissance" of the South was clearly under way.

Yet there was an odd disproportion to it, for while Wilson seemed to be thinking chiefly about poetry, the list above is heavily overbalanced by writers of fiction. Ireland, the country to which he aptly compared the South, had experienced its own renaissance two or three decades earlier; there, while eminent fiction was certainly created, the achievement in poetry was at least equally great. Like Ireland, the South had a rural way of life that was now under considerable strain, an oral culture that had survived in at least some corners of the country, a language that was identifiably but not unintelligibly different from that of the metropolitan culture, heroic traditions, and an obsession with its own past defeats and conquest. All of these qualities seemed to have encouraged the production of great poetry in Ireland, and one might have expected them to have the same effect in the South. T.S. Eliot, an authority in these matters, regarded the South as unusually fortunate in having genuine, surviving, and poetically usable traditions. Whereas Ireland gave the world Yeats, however, the South produced Faulkner. "In poetry and criticism the South, of course, is still behind," noted Howard Mumford Jones in the *Virginia Quarterly Review* for April 1930. In criticism the situation would soon be remedied by the very men whose poetry Wilson had reviewed two years earlier, but so far as poetry goes Jones might feel little reason to change his opinion today.

Indeed, the lyric and narrative poetry produced during the continuing literary renaissance in the South has been so much less impressive than the fiction that the anomaly cries out for explanation. The appearance of literary genius may be unpredictable and culturally inexplicable, but the directions that literary talent habitually follows—and how far it goes—are another matter. Not only has the South produced no Yeats, it has never given birth even to a Robert Frost, a poet of national stature closely identified with one region. Of the leading Fugitives themselves, Ransom had largely stopped writing poetry by 1928, while the young Tate had already written most of the poems by which he is known today. Both subsequently became far more influential and better-known as literary critics than they had ever been as poets. Indeed, with the exception of Warren, none of the Fugitives really made a career of poetry. Few Southern poets have ever devoted themselves to poetry as Yeats or Frost did, or as Faulkner and Eudora Welty devoted themselves to fiction. (James Dickey has announced his intention of doing so.) Fiction and criticism seem to be perennial distractions for the Southern poet in a way (or at least to a degree) that they had not been for British, Irish, or New England poets.

Why should this be so? It is doubtful that the South in the twentieth century has been any less receptive to poetry than other parts of the country. The leading Southern quarterlies have long been among the most prestigious markets for poetry, and Southern university presses issue more than their share of new poetry volumes. The Southern reading public is no more provincial than that of Ireland or northern New England, nor does the South exercise a less powerful hold on the literary imagination, as its achievements in fiction make plain. The reasons for its failure to produce more than a few works of poetry that are regarded as important outside the region must be sought both in the peculiarities of its own literary and cultural traditions and in the ambivalence that inevitably besets any serious poet who tries to resist the homogenized cosmopolitanism of modern high culture. In their defiant assertion of the local, the special, the untypical, Southern poets ironically furnish a paradigmatic case of this ambivalence and its literary consequences. Since it is futile to speculate about great poems that no one has succeeded in writing, the most practicable way of approaching the matter is to examine some of the best and most obviously Southern poems written during this century in respect to one narrow question: how their authors have given poetic form to the wealth of identifiably regional materials and attitudes.

So much criticism has already been devoted to the major Fugitives that one hesitates to go over such well-plowed ground again for fear of sinking up to one's waist. Most of the sympathetic critics, it is clear, have looked upon their regional identification as a source of strength, even of their main success as poets. To me, however, it appears that their relations with their region, of which they were all intensely conscious, were a problem they never resolved successfully as poets. (With their successes or failures as social thinkers I am not concerned.) The fact that Tate and Ransom never fulfilled the promise of the poems they had written in the 1920s, and that within a few years after publishing such a manifesto as *I'll Take My Stand* not only Tate and Ransom but Warren as well had moved away from the South, argues a desperate if honorable failure that has something to do with the region itself. This impression is reinforced by the continued failure of Southern poets after the Fugitives to use their region as writers must do who are to be considered of major significance beyond it. Of course the examination of a few poems proves little; but the weaknesses of some important poems may shed light on the whole enterprise of regional poetry in this century.

The Southern artist, wrote Donald Davidson in 1926, "is in a forbidding situation, and is overwhelmed by a set of complex inhibitions that make him extremely self-conscious in his attitude toward his own habitat. And the more completely he is aware of the phenomena of modern literature—the more nearly he approaches a perfection of his technical equipment—the greater these inhibitions will become." The reasons for this unhappy situation were hardly complimentary to the South and gave a far different picture of the artist's position from that of Wilson. Far from being an accepted member of a leisured community that valued art, Davidson argued, the artist was "an alien particle in the body politic," the heir to historical and social traditions that had been "mouthed over and cheapened" to the point where an artist of education and integrity could approach them only with the greatest wariness. As to the native intellectual life, "The Old South, as Allen Tate has observed, left no culture of ideas that the Southern writer can cheerfully use. . . . And, by contrast, fresh ideas, new modes, new philosophies come to him [the Southern artist] from every quarter but the South." Complaining that these reasons would make it very difficult for the South to produce a Frost or a Hardy, Davidson then put his finger on a fundamental dilemma of Southern poetry: "The deliberately southern Southerner runs the risk of being emptily local and sentimental; the inhibited modern, taking extra care to be non-sentimental, becomes splenetic, austere, remote."[1] Too close an identification with one's material was as bad as too detached a relation.

That these were the two extremes to be avoided all the major Fugitives agreed; that in managing to avoid them one might spend all one's energies producing poetry that was merely safe—academically passionate, or cautiously chauvinistic—was a possibility of which they were uncomfortably aware. During the first phase of Fugitive poetry, while the group was still in existence, the emphasis was on avoiding the first danger—"THE FUGITIVE flees from nothing faster than from the high-caste Brahmins of the Old South," declared the first issue of their magazine. Later on it was the analytic intellect that posed the greater danger, dissolving the institutions of an ordered society and sundering such educated men as themselves from the regional life in which they wished to feel at home. (This view of the abstract "modern" mind they shared with Yeats, who had an equal horror of rootlessness and an even more idealized view of the pre-industrial past.) By that time, however, Ransom, of whom Davidson was probably thinking when he wrote his last clause, had largely given up the writing of poetry.

That Ransom's insistent irony masks without really hiding an affection for the mythical Southern past is obvious, but the reasons for the transparent mask are less so.[2] In several of his most famous poems children and animals die, a fact that has led some commentators to regard him as acerbically unromantic. Since such deaths are usually among the most potent sources of sentimentality in literature, however, Ransom's irony, his use of the unexpected word or the mildly shocking humorous phrase, enables him to have it both ways—to be simultaneously nostalgic and tough-mindedly modern. This game with fire is played with great skill, but it is by nature a limited technique whose effects are quickly exhausted. In "Dead Boy," for example, is the infant cousin whose "foul subtraction" gives rise to such real and make-believe grief merely an occasion for contrast between the poet's detached perceptions ("pig with a pasty face") and the sentimental ones of the "county kin," or is there something more than a child or a single family whose death is being mourned here? Apparently the latter, for once dead the child shows his "forbears' antique lineaments," and his death leaves "Virginia's aged tree" without branches. Yet as a symbol for a dying tradition or way of life, the boy is singularly inappropriate. His only share in that tradition is genetic, and his age raises irrelevant associations. The Old South as Victorianized dead child is, indeed, grotesque. To say that such considerations are irrelevant in evaluating the poem is to imply either that it carries no symbolic suggestion about the traditional South (in which case Ransom is teasing us with "Virginia's aged tree" and its "sapless limbs") or that in this kind of poetry a symbol need be only superficially appropriate and may be used merely for emotional effect. In either case, there is an intellectual defect in Ransom's use of a regional theme.

"Old Mansion" is equally rueful about the decline of Southern tradition and much more explicit about the poet's failure to enter into that tradition. The poet, "an intruder," approaches the old house "with careful innocence," fascinated by its age, grandeur and legend but deeply conscious of himself as an outsider.

> It was a Southern manor. One need hardly imagine
> Towers, white monoliths, or even ivied walls;
> But sufficient state if its peacock *was* a pigeon;
> Where no courts held, but grave rites and funerals.

Alas, the building and grounds are decayed, reminding the "watchful heart" that the house and its tradition are approaching dissolution. It is in fact a *château moralisé* whose present state suggests not only the graceful past but the unknown future—"And one had best hurry to enter it if one can."

The poet knocks bravely at the door, only to discover that the decay of tradition is not confined to externals; the mistress is old, ill, and—worse—lacking in hospitality, and he is sent on his way. The tradition the house represents will remain unrecorded in its decline, for "no annalist went in to the lord or the peons"; some day in the future an archeologist will "finger the bits of shard" and reconstruct a way of life as best he can. For the poet, there will never be the knowledge of what life was like inside. Indeed, that is itself the lesson of the experience; the failure is not merely or even primarily the decay of the house, but the poet's inability to enter.

> But on retreating I saw myself in the token,
> How loving from my foreign weed the feather curled
> On the languid air; and I went with courage shaken
> To dip, alas, into some unseemlier world.

When the poet feels himself so consistently to be outside the traditions that inspire him, he has little choice but to cloak both his affection and his chagrin in ironies and to mock himself as a man out of his proper time and place. A poet who feels this way is by definition unlikely to embody much of his region in verse. If he avoids being splenetic, in Davidson's phrase, his work is almost certain to be austere and remote, as a poem like "Antique Harvesters" is deliberately remote from any

real South past or present. In most of his verse Ransom is both concerned to distance himself from his material (whether ostensibly regional or not) and regretful at not being able to enter into it more
fully. Out of such an ambivalence poetry could come, but not confident or major poetry. When the balance eventually tipped one way or
the other, as it was always threatening to do, the irony that was at the
heart of Ransom's verse became impossible. "*Patriotism* has nearly
eaten me up," he wrote to Tate in 1936, "and I've got to get out of
it." His abandonment of poetry and his subsequent repudiation of
agrarianism were not unrelated events.

Of all the Fugitives, it is probably Robert Penn Warren who has
come closest, in his long and distinguished post-Fugitive career, to
writing major poetry. Much of his very large output of verse is not
Southern in setting, though most of his work has been unified by certain themes that have come to be regarded as typically Southern, such
as a sense of original sin, a strong feeling of identification with the
land, and the persistence of the past. It is more than usually difficult
and unfair to represent such a poet by one poem, but a work of Warren's maturity that embodies all of these themes in a Southern setting
is "The Ballad of Billie Potts" (1944, quoted here from the revised version in Warren's *Selected Poems 1923-1975*). That, like other poems by
Warren, it also embodies some of the same problems that afflicted
Ransom is compelling testimony to the difficulty the best Southern
poets have had in making regional materials both convincing in themselves and at the same time transcendent of merely regional concerns.[3]

As its title implies, "The Ballad of Billie Potts" is an attempt to render Southern life of a level considerably less exalted than the lives of
Ransom's aged or infant aristocrats. Set in the "land between the riv-
ers" of western Kentucky, it is based on the ancient folktale of the
exiled son who returns in disguise and is murdered by his own parents,
a version of which Warren had heard from an aged relative when he
was a child. The poem begins in a loose ballad style appropriate to its
peasant characters and the story-telling tradition in which it presumably falls:

> Big Billie Potts was big and stout
> In the land between the rivers
> His shoulders were wide and his gut stuck out

> Like a croker of nubbins and his holler and shout
> Made the bob-cat shiver and the black-jack leaves shake
> In the section between the rivers.
> He would slap you on your back and laugh.

The other two major characters, Mrs. Potts and Little Billie, are introduced similarly, with about an equal number of dialect words and phrases which, if their use seems slightly self-conscious, undeniably fit the people who are being described (Little Billie, for example, is "A clabber-headed bastard with snot in his nose").

Thus far the imitation of a folk ballad has been maintained with consistency, but having introduced his characters Warren immediately breaks off into a chorus-like commentary on the place which is not in ballad form and has no direct connection with his story. This commentary, like similar sections throughout the poem, is enclosed in parentheses to set it off from the ballad proper. The level of sophistication and sensitivity in these passages, obviously, is much higher than that of the characters in the story:

> (It is not hard to see the land, what it was.
> Low hills and oak. The fetid bottoms where
> The slough uncoiled and in the tangled cane,
> Where no sun comes, the muskrat's astute face
> Was lifted to the yammering jay; then dropped.
> A cabin where the shagbark stood and the
> Magnificent tulip-tree; both now are gone. . . .

Having read thus far, one begins to wonder why the author felt that a commentary so at variance with the tone of his ballad was necessary even at the risk of the poem's integrity. This feeling of unease grows as one reads the rest of the work.

The ballad proper resumes with a nine-line section on Big Billie's entrepreneurial activities—he built an inn and prospered—which is immediately followed by another meditative passage, this one about time ("Their names are like the leaves, but are forgot"). A longer section of ballad makes it clear that Big Billie's prosperity is partly the result of highway robbery: he arranges for his richer guests to be ambushed after they leave the inn. Then the plot (which has not really begun yet) is interrupted once again by more commentary on time, now rather reminiscent of Eliot:

> (There was a beginning but you cannot see it.
> There will be an end but you cannot see it.
> They will not turn their faces to you though you call,
> Who pace a logic merciless as light. . . .)

The story itself can be quickly summarized: Little Billie is sent out with a message about a stranger who looks promising; being "full of piss and vinegar," he decides to waylay the stranger alone and thereby prove himself a man. But the stranger is no fool, and Billie ends up with a wound in his arm. To avoid further trouble with the stranger or his friends, Big Billie sends his son out west with two hundred dolars in gold and a fast horse. That is the last his parents hear of him for nearly ten years. When he returns he is rich and mature, his appearance disguised by a long black beard; he decides to take advantage of his unrecognizability by visiting his parents incognito, forgetting their usual treatment of strangers who appear to have money. When Little Billie bends down to drink at his parents' spring, they kill him with a hatchet. Later, when told that the man who visited them was their son, they refuse to believe it until they have dug him up and identified him by a small black birthmark under his left breast.

Their discovery of this mark is the end of the ballad proper, but it is both preceded and followed by long meditative passages about time and identity which, as before, have no direct connection with the action, though they address a wandering figure who finds that his identity is somehow tied up in the place from which he came.

> Therefore you tried to remember when you had last had
> Whatever it was you had lost,
> And you decided to retrace your steps from that point,
> But it was a long way back.
> It was, nevertheless, absolutely essential to make the effort,
> And since you had never been a man to be deterred by
>   difficult circumstances,
> You came back.
> For there is no place like home.

What we have in this passage, I think, is the same problem as in the whole poem: a mixture of voices that cannot be effectively harmonized. The sixth line above is deliberately pedantic; the eighth is a cliché no serious writer could use without conscious irony, although in fact it comes very close to embodying the meaning of Warren's parable about rootedness and identity. The most serious defect of the poem, however, is that the parable is not self-explanatory. In order to make it bear the meanings he wishes it to convey, Warren must continually depart from both the story and the ballad form to point out meanings that it cannot be trusted to communicate by itself. He chose to use a regional folk tale (or at least a regional version of a widespread folk tale) and unsophisticated characters who were recognizably of their time and place; he chose also to be faithful to the literary heritage of the place by more or less following a traditional ballad form. Having done so, however, he was stuck with a plot susceptible of numerous interpretations (Albert Camus's use of it in *Le Malentendu,* for example, is far different) and characters who were so much less reflective and articulate than their author that they could not plausibly voice the major concerns Warren wished to embody in the poem. Hence the continual interruptions became unavoidable because the regional material would not in itself do what Warren wanted. The ballad itself, instead of genuinely bearing the universal meanings that were central in Warren's mind, is simply an inadequate regional illustration of them in action, expressed with unintentional condescension in a form which he abandons whenever he wishes to tell his reader something that is over the heads of his characters. Like Ransom, he never really shares the world of those characters—not because their world is exclusive and exalted, in this case, but because it is narrow and has denied them the scope either to express or to recognize those aspects of their own existences that a twentieth-century poet finds important.

The most sensational and traumatic event in Southern history, the one that has most haunted Southern writers since it occurred, is the Civil War. Here, one might think, is a rich basis for a poetic mythology—a genuinely shared set of emotions, stories, symbols, and attitudes—even more available to the Southern poet than the "Romantic Ireland" of 1798 was to Yeats, either for allusion or for direct treatment. A great many poems have in fact been written about the Civil War, including two of the most celebrated Fugitive works—Allen Tate's "Ode to the Confederate Dead" (first published in 1928 and afterwards laboriously revised) and Donald Davidson's "Lee in the Mountains" (1938). How have these two major Southern poets dealt with the Civil War for a twentieth-century audience?

"It is pretty certain," Tate wrote in the *Nation* (28 October 1925) while living in New York, "that the Southern variety of American writer must first see himself, if at all, through other eyes. For he of all Americans is privy to the emotions founded in the state of knowing oneself to be a foreigner at home." A decade later Cleanth Brooks, writing on "The Modern Southern Poet and Tradition" in the *Virginia Quarterly Review* (April 1935), explained in part why the Southern poet was so peculiarly foreign to both the past and present of his region: "The Old South cannot exist in the mind of the modern Southerner apart from its non-existence in the present." The Southern poet must "mediate his account of the Old South through a consciousness of the present; that is, of its present non-existence." Similarly, his awareness of the present was colored by his sense of the past. Only by thus balancing past and present could he avoid both sentimentality and mere local color. It might be supposed that Tate's "Ode to the Confederate Dead" (here quoted from the revised version in *Collected Poems*) fulfills this prescription better than almost any other Southern poem. Actually, however, neither past nor present is quite what it seems in this much analyzed poem, whose tone is considerably more private than its title would suggest.

Tate and most of his commentators notwithstanding, there is nothing in the poem about either solipsism or narcissism as properly understood,[4] neither of which is a likely cause for despair. On the contrary, the speaker is only too aware that other people besides himself do exist (he repeatedly uses *we* to give his remarks a general application) and have in the past sometimes been heroes. He is also far from loving himself; the contrast between present and past leads him very near to self-hatred. If the speaker could really "create the world in the act of perceiving it" (Tate's definition of solipsism), it is unlikely that he would create a heroic tradition which implicitly reproves him, or that he would think about it as he does in the poem. Nor, if his real problem were the kind of skepticism about causes that many in the 1920s re-garded as typically modern, would he feel his situation to be so unsatis-factory. There is nothing in the poem to suggest that the speaker feels any doubt about either the Confederate cause or the principle of heroic action. On the contrary, his problem is that he lives in a world with no scope or opportunity for such action—a world that sees only "the leaves / Flying, plunge and expire" and in which "mute speculation" has usurped the place of action.

Tate's speaker is a visitor from the Waste Land whose difficulties seem to arise not from his own subjectivity but from the objective facts of his situation—it is the 1920s, not the 1860s; society and war have changed. (Like many modernists of the 1920s, Tate may well have thought the change permanent; Fascism, Spain, the Battle of Britain and other instances of heroic commitment were still in the unimagina-ble future.) It is his own age the speaker is at war with; although he is affected by its attitudes sufficiently to speak of "arrogant circum-stance" and the "immoderate past," he is not critical of the past to any significant degree. Rather it is "we"—"modern 'intellectual man,'" as Tate identified him—who are at fault for believing that

> Night is the beginning and the end
> And in between the ends of distraction
> Waits mute speculation, the patient curse
> That stones the eyes, or like the jaguar leaps
> For his own image in a jungle pool, his victim.

Speculation may leap, but the speaker has no intention of doing so, and it is clear that he does not really share the beliefs which he ascribes to his contemporaries. What he lacks is not so much the will of his anon-ymous Confederates—though he rather patronizingly assumes himself to be much more learned and thoughtful than they were—but their cause and opportunities for heroism. (He might turn out to lack their courage and skills if put to the test, but that is not an issue in the poem.)

This is what the poem seems to say, but there is a tone of despair that is far in excess of mere regret at having been born out of one's proper time. One's birthdate is after all not a matter of choice—or only so for a solipsist—and to blame oneself for it is scarcely reasonable. There is a private discouragement below the surface of the poem which is ineffectively dramatized by the contrast between the "modern" mind and that of the Confederate soldier. Indeed, the Confederate soldier is merely a type of heroic action, a disembodied abstraction. He is half of a very crude dichotomy, the other half being passive speculation. As in "Billie Potts," regional material has been used here to symbolize issues with which it really has nothing to do and which it does not convincingly represent.[5] Donald Davidson's criticism of the poem in manuscript, expressed in a letter to Tate in 1927, is essentially correct: "The Confederate dead become a peg on which you hang an argument whose lines, however sonorous and beautiful in a strict proud way, leave me wondering why you wrote a poem on the subject at all, since in effect you say (and I suspect you are speaking partly to me) that no poem can be written on such a subject. Your *Elegy* [the original title] is not for the Confederate dead, but for your own dead emotion, or mine (*you* think)."[6]

Davidson's emotion was not dead, and if he was strongly aware of the dangers that lay in trying to use the "mouthed over and cheapened" traditions of Southern heroism in poetry, his feeling towards those traditions was so much stronger than those of his fellow Fugitives that he was determined to try where he thought Tate had failed. Working on the collection that became *Lee in the Mountains* (1938), he wrote to John Gould Fletcher: "I have been trying to see whether a poet can deal with 'confederate' material without turning it into personal poetry as Allen does in his 'Ode.'"[7] The search for a "usable past" led him not to Confederates in their glory, however, but to the aftermath of defeat.

"Lee in the Mountains" is, more than "Ode to the Confederate Dead," a dramatic monologue. Here, however, the speaker is not a modern man but General Lee; the past speaks for itself. The past (in this case the last five years of Lee's life) is the present, the twentieth century the future—a reversal of Tate's procedure that makes the poem a genuine work of the historical imagination. In it General Lee—now plain Robert Lee—walks across the campus of Washington College to his office to edit the memoirs of his long-dead father. He thinks of his father's grave, which he had visited during the war, and of the war itself:

He would have his say, but I shall not have mine. . . .
The rest must pass to men who never knew
(But on a written page) the strike of armies,
And never heard the long Confederate cry
Charge through the muzzling smoke or saw the bright
Eyes of the beardless boys go up to death.

Nowhere in this poem is there any irony, and instead of distancing himself from his historical material the way Tate or Warren would have done, Davidson appears to endorse everything that he gives General Lee to say. The effect is almost the opposite of what happens in Tate's "Ode," for whereas Tate used the past merely as a symbol for other things, Davidson's procedure very nearly obliterates the present. It is almost as if the poet and his century had been swallowed up by "old Virginia times now faint and gone, / The hurt of all that was and cannot be." Almost, but not quite. For Lee's vision of the future is recognizably that of the modern agrarian poet whose view of the past is properly influenced by his awareness of the present, just as Lee himself evaluates the peaceful present by reference to the past:

Was it for this
That on an April day we stacked our arms
Obedient to a soldier's trust? To lie
Ground by the heels of little men,
Forever maimed, defeated, lost, impugned?

The only alternative, seemingly, was guerrilla warfare in the mountains. Lee had urged such a course upon Jefferson Davis, who had refused his permission. Such a war might still be possible even after Appomattox (Davidson's poem "Sanctuary" seems to envision something very similar), but Lee refuses to order it, not out of a desire to be conciliatory but apparently in the faith that the blood of the Confederate dead will itself lead to some indescribable redemption if the South keeps faith with them and with God. The fine ending of the poem is Lee's counsel to the future, and also Davidson's:

And in His might He waits,
Brooding within the certitude of time,

To bring this lost forsaken valor
And the fierce faith undying
And the love quenchless
To flower among the hills to which we cleave,
To fruit upon the mountains whither we flee,
Never forsaking, never denying
His children and His children's children forever
Unto all generations of the faithful heart.

Whatever evaluation one makes of "Lee in the Mountains," it is a far cry from anything Ransom, Tate, or Warren produced. Its chief virtues, from the standpoint of effective regional writing, are that it is not condescending toward its material and does not use the regional simply as an illustration of something else more important to its writer. Its defect is that it is *too* resolutely historical. Little attempt is made to show Lee as a universal type of nobility in defeat, and there are few concessions for the outland reader who either knows only the main outline of Lee's life or cares about the Civil War only as it reflects broader concerns. To anyone who does not already regard the South's defeat as a tragedy, the poem has little to say. It is a work of art so quixotically regional as to be of only regional significance. [8]

I suspect that by 1938 Davidson would not have regarded this as a very telling criticism, but the earlier Davidson who was troubled by the self-consciousness of Southern artists believed that good regional writing must transcend provincial concerns. The two extremes to be avoided, we may recall, were the "emptily local and sentimental" and the "splenetic, austere, remote." "Lee in the Mountains" is not quite the former, just as Tate's "Ode" is not quite the latter—they are both too good for that—but neither keeps altogether clear of these extremes. Of the two most famous modern poems evoking the Confederacy, neither makes a really satisfactory use of the most potent historical material the South has to offer, and neither offers a solution to the major dilemmas of Southern—or modern—poetry.

The most powerful twentieth-century poets in English have been, by and large, those who could seize hold of regional landscapes and traditions and use them convincingly as mirrors for larger concerns:

Hardy, Yeats, Frost, the Eliot of *Four Quartets,* the early Lowell. Southern poets early in the century would seem to have been granted a promising background (if not a very useful literary heritage) for similar kinds of achievement, and for a time it seemed as though they might make the most of their opportunities. In April 1922, a few months before the first issue of the *Fugitive* appeared, the editors of *Poetry* devoted a special issue to the South in which DuBose Heyward and Hervey Allen prophesied: "Despite some vigorous assertions to the contrary, it seems as if Southern poetry were going to be decidedly regional in spirit, with a quick human appeal but strongly local in tone—poetry of and about places."

For reasons I have been examining, however, Southern poets have rarely been able to make the most effective use of their regional material, with the result that Southern poetry, like regional poetry in general over the last few decades, has been somewhat stunted. Of course some poets born in the South have dealt with the difficulty by ignoring regional material and attitudes largely or altogether—Randall Jarrell and A.R. Ammons come to mind as examples—but in so doing they have lost the advantages of place and tradition as well as the disadvantages. Commenting in 1935 on a renaissance that had already reached its peak, Ransom acknowledged: "Suddenly, and in some way connected with the force of social decay and modernism, the prose fiction has come abundantly to life; but the verse is not yet, on the whole, alive." His attempts to explain this regrettable situation did not go very far, however. "There is lacking in the equipment of our writers a sufficient aesthetic of poetry," he declared murkily, "and that is all the cause that is required." Then he turned jocularly to make what was in fact a more penetrating point: "There is little distinctively Southern poetry . . . because one of the peculiarities of the region is that it still conceives poetry as an adolescent function, and all adolescents are more or less alike."[9] Another way of putting this might be to say that while the regional popular culture gave some support to the writing of fiction (story-telling being a tradition that still survived), it gave none to the writing of poetry, with the result that the Southern poet inevitably felt more alienated from the region about which he was attempting to write than either the Southern novelist or, say, the New England poet. Very little good poetry had been written in the South during any pre-

vious period, which made it difficult for Southern poets in the twentieth century to appeal from popular culture to a more elevated but still
native literary tradition in which they might have found strength. The
absence of a single cultural capital for the whole South—a Dublin or a
Boston—isolated poets even more. It is hardly surprising that the Fugitives felt the need to band together in a group, or that within a few
years after they disbanded most of them either gave up poetry or left
the South. The combination of self-consciousness about using regional
materials that Davidson had pointed out and lack of support from any
significant elements of the culture they were attempting to celebrate
was a powerful demoralizing force for the Fugitives and their successors.

In 1936 Warren, aware of the problems but unwilling to give up on
regionalism, compiled "Some Don'ts for Literary Regionalists"[10] that,
read with hindsight, are extremely illuminating about regional poetry
written both before and since. The "Don'ts" were six in number and,
in abbreviated form, ran as follows: (1) "Regionalism is not quaintness
and local color and folklore, for those things when separated from a
functional idea are merely a titillation of the reader's sentimentality or
snobbishness"; (2) "Regionalism based on the literary exploitation of a
race or society that has no cultural continuity with our own tends to
be false and precious"; (3) "Regionalism does not necessarily imply an
emphasis on the primitive or underprivileged character. . . . There is a
literature of false primitivism as well as the literature of superficial sophistication"; (4) "Regionalism does not mean that a writer should re-
linquish any resource of speculation or expression that he has managed
to achieve. . . . There is no compulsion in regionalism that a modern
poet should write fake folk-ballads or that a novelist should cultivate
illiteracy as a virtue"; (5) "Regionalism does not mean that literature
is tied to its region for appreciation"; and finally, (6) "Even literary regionalism is more than a literary matter, and is not even primarily a literary matter."

All of the poets I have been talking about were aware from the start
of the dangers of mere local color; to all of them regionalism has been
more than a literary matter. The most common problems have arisen
in trying to marry the "functional idea" to the regional setting and
characters, and the attempt to do so has led most of our poets to vi-

olate more than one of these sensible injunctions. The novelist, even if he is not a Faulkner, has enormous advantages over the poet in using regional materials for universal themes; he can characterize at length, bring in a whole society of diverse people, externalize a variety of attitudes through them, and show development over long periods of time. Since family and community ties, violent conflict, and a sense of historical change are themes that most Southern writers have found important, it is no wonder that the novelists have managed to achieve more with them than the poets have.

The self-consciousness of the relatively sophisticated poet before his native traditions was something that Warren acknowledged obliquely. Hawthorne, he suggested, did not have to "reason or will himself into his regionalism, into appropriate relation to his place and its past and present." The modern writer was not so fortunate; he must seize by effort traditions that would have been his birthright in previous centuries. (Tate had earlier said much the same thing, echoing Eliot on the difficulty of the task.)

It is often forgotten in discussions of poetic regionalism that both Yeats and Frost were citizens of their regions more by choice than by birth. The labor they spent in constructing usable versions of local tradition for themselves was not inhibited by close childhood association with the region and its actual mores. Yeats, the son of an English-descended Protestant artist, spent much of his life in England and deliberately revived forgotten episodes of Irish myth and history for poetic use. Frost, born in San Francisco and named for the Confederate general whose years of retirement Davidson would later celebrate, was eleven years old before he ever saw New England and spent much effort acquiring the appearance of a native son. Both benefited enormously in that the regional material and attitudes they used so effectively had not been reduced to cliché or commonplace for them by the time they were old enough to write. Neither was fully native to his region, although neither was altogether alien. Similarly Poe, the one Southern poet of indisputably major importance, is the most disputably Southern. It may be that such an ambiguous status, leading to a deliberate identification with the region, encourages the production of poetry in which the local will stand convincingly for the world. If so, it is unfortunate that the South has had relatively few literary immigrants of the necessary impressionable age.

The mixed success of such an ambitious attempt at regional poetry as we have been examining, together with the general decline of convincing regional poetry elsewhere in the last forty years, are an indication that the dikes of the local have not furnished much of a barrier to the tide of cosmopolitanism even for those who, like the leading modernist poets, spent their lives attacking the rootlessness of modern culture. With a few exceptions, twentieth-century poets have themselves been so dominated by analytic, urbane, and international habits of thought that their arguments for rootedness have had a curiously abstract quality. Modern poetry has lavishly praised people who had their roots in Confucian China, medieval France, renaissance Italy, or even eighteenth-century Ireland. It has never quite gotten over the suspicion that people with their roots in a distinct corner of the contemporary world are merely provincial. This suspicion is, of course, both a cause and a consequence of the cultural homogenization that I mentioned at the beginning of this chapter, a homogenization to which the most central twentieth-century poets have contributed even by their manner of deploring it.

SEVEN

The Place of Poetry

If the poetry of the rest of this century takes the line of
development which seems to me, reviewing the progress of
poetry through the last three centuries, the right course,
it will discover new and more elaborate patterns of a
diction now established. . . . It might also avoid the danger
of a *servitude* to colloquial speech and to current jargon.
It might also learn that the music of verse is strongest
in poetry which has a definite meaning expressed
in the properest words.

T.S. Eliot, "Milton II"

Many causes can be adduced for the decline in the poetic audience that
seems to have been most rapid between the 1920s and the 1950s, the
period that David Perkins describes as having been dominated by
"high modernism." As we have seen, the crisis of poetry did not begin
in the twentieth century; it goes back at least to the late eighteenth.
But the size and enthusiasm of poetry's audience did not begin to
dwindle until near the end of the nineteenth century. On the contrary,
during the first part of that century they even grew. Walter Jackson
Bate has described the status of poetry with nineteenth-century publishers and readers:

> If a poem did catch on, it brought returns that now seem to us
> incredible. . . . Longman gave Tom Moore, for *Lalla Rookh,*
> what would now amount to $50,000, and Murray offered the
> same sum to George Crabbe for *Tales of the Hall* and half as
> much to Byron for a single canto of *Childe Harold.* A generation
> later, Longfellow's *Courtship of Myles Standish* was to sell ten
> thousand copies in one day in London alone, though the subject
> was not particularly familiar to English readers and though the
> novel had long since become the dominant form for narrative
> and was indeed fast becoming the dominant literary form gener-

ally. These were exceptions, of course. Any one volume was a gamble. But there were plenty of publishers ready to take it.[1]

With a few notable exceptions whom I shall take up presently, the poets of today do not expect to pay their rent out of royalties, let alone to buy *palazzos* in Venice. They are far more apt to quote ruefully Milton's dictum about "fit audience though few," and to question in their darker moments whether even so modest a readership still exists to be captured. Some of the causes behind this drastic change of fortune, such as the fact that higher education has become (thanks in part to T.H. Huxley) much more technical and less literary than it once was, have little to do with the practices of poets, although people educated along such lines may have been encouraged in their feeling that poetry had nothing important to say to them by the privateness and obscurity of so much modernist and post-modernist verse. The claims of poetry to be the best source of knowledge about human nature and experience came to seem unconvincing to most readers in the age of the social sciences, whose collective name at least carried the promise of greater system and rigor. Poetry came more and more to seem, in Gatsby's endlessly illuminating phrase, "just personal," inherently an esoteric entertainment ("superior amusement," in Eliot's words) of no real or public importance. The idea of a public poetry came to seem, in fact, a contradiction in terms. Poets' use of common language at a time when every field of knowledge took increasing pride in its own jargon merely confirmed these suspicions of unimportance. Simultaneously, in an egalitarian society membership in a small isolated minority of poets or readers, whether self-defined as an élite or not, ceased to be exhilarating and became simply demoralizing.

During the same period when changes in the educational system were transforming the outlook of the highly educated, equally important shifts were occurring in the emotional and connotative values of the language, of which poets were equally guiltless. For while Pound and Eliot were laboriously engaged in purifying the dialect of the tribe, that dialect was being increasingly corrupted by the manipulative usages of advertising and mass communications. One result was a heightening of skepticism toward certain kinds of abstract or emotive words that poets had traditionally relied on. "Poetic language," as S.I.

Hayakawa has sagely observed, "is used so constantly and relentlessly for the purposes of salesmanship that it has become almost impossible to say anything with enthusiasm or joy or conviction without running into the danger of sounding as if you were selling something." How could the poet write feelingly about green fields in spring if a large part of the audience half-consciously associated them with toilet paper? How talk affectingly about love to any but the most unsophisticated when love was the staple of advertising everything from children's toothpaste to Geritol? Or freedom and country in an age of televised wars and political campaigns? The result, according to Hayakawa, is that "For at least a generation there have been no poets—not even Robert Frost or Carl Sandburg—who could communicate with as large a portion of the literate public as Tennyson and Longfellow did in their time."[2] (In Wales, a noteworthy provincial contrast, poetry continued to involve the whole community in part because, as Richard Jones declares, "the Welsh language . . . has been untouched by copywriters' plastic ecstasy or by the ironies and cynical undertones that make it quite difficult to be sincere and eloquent in modern English without sounding absurd."[3])

Hayakawa seems to think not only that no poet of any sophistication can use traditional symbols with the ease that was possible a hundred years ago, which is true, but also that sales resistance to such symbols has destroyed their appeal to readers, which is much less true. The irony of such poets as Eliot, Auden, and Richard Wilbur was a constructive attempt to avoid what seemed to be a culture-wide commercialized sentimentality and thereby resist the total conquest of public discourse by institutions whose sole interest in it was as a medium of manipulation. But people who lacked the cultural resources or experience to resist being manipulated naturally did not understand this kind of irony, and it is hardly surprising that the sort of contemporary poetry that appealed (and appeals) to them was precisely the sort that manipulated most deliberately—that was, in effect, a product of the world of advertising. Poetry of the greatest cultural importance has historically dealt with those aspects of reality in which people found their identity and security. But a society in which many people find their chief security and sense of meaning through commercial products, from the possession of certain objects, will produce great advertising, not great poetry; the things most available for use as symbols are not of enough long-term importance to support serious art. The poet then may feel faced with the choice of being either trivial (producing a literary equivalent of pop art) or so outside the main concerns of his age as to seem irrelevant to all but a small minority of potential readers.

That the serious poet's isolation and impotence are at least partly his own doing, however, is suggested by a fact that most literary commentators have overlooked: despite presumed competition from prose and electronic forms of entertainment, poetry written on and for the lowest levels of literary sophistication continues to flourish today. Rod McKuen, a few similar poets such as Lois Wyse, and the authors of popular song lyrics (than which nothing could be poetically more conservative in structure and content) are rich and famous, as adulated as medieval troubadours in what most critics regard as subliterary circles.[4] Indeed, McKuen's publishers (Random House) claim preposterously that he is "the bestselling and most widely read poet of all times." Further, they add somewhat anticlimactically, "he is the bestselling living author writing in any hardcover medium today."

Even allowing for the pardonable delirium of a publisher who has seen poetry pay, McKuen has probably sold more books than any other twentieth-century English or American poet: something over ten million in the six years preceding the publication of his thirteenth collection in 1975. It is a revealing sign of the times that in the face of such evident prosperity, his blurb-writer should administer the *coup de grace* to any doubts about McKuen's eminence by adding that "his poetry is taught and studied in schools, colleges, universities, and seminaries [!] throughout the world." In fact, while his books sell well to undergraduates, his poems are included in few anthologies; the most comprehensive and academically favored collection of modern verse, published by Norton, does not even mention him. McKuen's verse is what poetry written deliberately for a mass audience has been since the time of Martin Tupper: easily understood on first reading or hearing, stale and conventional in its phrasing and imagery, heavily sentimental, and filled with uncomplicated messages about life. Perhaps his chief claim to notability is that he saw the possibility of making poems into what are simultaneously commercial products and advertisements for emotions, written for an audience whose education in affective language has come largely from advertising and popular music. (It is worth pointing out, in the light of Hayakawa's thesis, that McKuen came to poetry after writing psychological-warfare scripts during the Korean War.) Practically all of his verse is about love or nature. He produces approximately a book a year.

It is not, therefore, primarily the uneducated or the half-educated who have stopped reading or otherwise consuming poetry. It is the literate and sophisticated—practically all of them, that is, who are not professional students of literature. No doubt "popular" poetry has always commanded a larger share of the total audience than that which caters to the more discerning; but the present situation, in which serious contemporary poetry has virtually no audience at all outside the English departments, is the unprecedented result of a collaboration between historical forces and the practices of twentieth-century poets themselves. That state of affairs demands more thorough consideration than it has yet received, despite the fact that the investigator is forced into so many risky areas of conjecture and supposition about an audience whose only certain characteristic is its disappearance.

It is doubtful that the demands of the educated public changed nearly so much as the practice of serious poets in the early twentieth century. Bate, speaking again of nineteenth-century verse, declares that its "openness of idiom . . . prevents the assumption, whether affected or genuinely despondent, that [popularity and artistic greatness] are mutually exclusive—and prevents it despite the deterministic arguments . . . about the modern split between 'sophisticated' and 'popular' art."[5] The much-mentioned difficulty and pessimism of so much modern verse are not the fundamental problem; Browning was difficult, Swinburne and Hardy pessimistic. The fact that it is difficult in unprecedented ways is more significant and points to what may be the most important fact about much twentieth-century verse: because of radical technical innovation and the impulse to render details with unparalleled emphasis, it is simply not what the common reader has been led for many centuries to regard as poetry. Riding and Graves in 1927 saw this problem as a disagreement

between the reading public and the modernist poet over the definition of clearness. Both agree that perfect clearness is the end of poetry, but the reading public insists that no poetry is clear except what it can understand at a glance; the modernist poet insists that the clearness of which the poetic mind is capable demands thought and language of a far greater sensitiveness and complexity than the enlarged reading public will permit it to use. To remain true to his conception of what poetry is, he has therefore to run the risk of seeming obscure or freakish, of having no reading public; even of writing what the reading public refuses to call poetry, in order to be a poet.[6]

Whether most modernist poets in practice agreed "that perfect clearness is the end of poetry," or whether the educated public really demanded such superficiality, is open to considerable doubt. It could also be maintained that the gap between "sophisticated" and "popular" poetry of which Bate speaks became an unbridgeable chasm when many of the modernists and their successors abandoned some indispensable ideas about the forms and functions of poetry: that it should illuminate rather than simply mirror experience; that it should discriminate those aspects of experience which are lastingly important from those which are trivial or transient; that while it may be difficult, it ought not to be pedantic or obscurely private; and that its language and structure are more formal than those of prose. The fact that in England, where modernist assumptions were less triumphant than in America, the decline in audience has also been less suggests that modernist efforts to "resuscitate the dead art of poetry" (Pound's phrase of 1920, then premature) achieved the opposite of their purpose so far as gaining readers was concerned. A poet whose work is read exclusively by professional students of literature can hardly be judged successful in restoring the cultural status of his art.

Readers of William Heyen's interesting contemporary survey *American Poets in 1976*, a collection of essays and recent poems by twenty-nine representative figures, will, it is fair to say, find the principles I have listed above in short supply. They have been increasingly regarded as quaint antiques since about 1915, when Pound formulated his rules for the imagistic poem. The most obvious result today is a demoralized solipsism that is one of the more depressing features of contemporary poetry. "I'll never have an audience of even fifty people who truly care about my poems," Mr. Heyen complains; ". . . all I can hope to do is write poems that please *me*."[7] Raised to the level of principle, solipsism led in the 1950s to the confessional poem, one of whose originators, Delmore Schwartz, justified it as an inevitable result of the poet's isolation: "Since the only life available to the poet as a man of culture has been the cultivation of his own sensibility, that is the only subject available to him, if we may assume that a poet can only write about subjects of which he has an absorbing experience in every way."[8] When the poet finds himself capable of writing only for and about himself, the decline of poetry as a cultural force is complete. By our own spirits are we deified, as Wordsworth said; but thereof come in the end despondency and madness.

Poetry, unlike the novel, has never been a literary form associated with a single social class. Different social classes, however, have always had different kinds of poetry catering to their different interests, tastes, and levels of sophistication. (It is obvious that the notion of class as defining levels of literary taste is an approximation at any period and becomes less satisfactory as we approach the present.) Regardless of the level of sophistication for which it was intended, however, almost all non-satirical poetry written before 1800 dealt with one or more of five broad areas in human experience: love, death, religion, war, and external nature. Around 1800 Wordsworth succeeded in adding a sixth: recollection of childhood. The efforts of many of his successors to demonstrate that *all* human experiences are equally fit subjects for poetry ("Anything is good material for poetry. Anything," declares William Carlos Williams; "We will talk of everything sooner or later," boasts Robert Creeley in Mr. Heyen's book[9]), and at the same time to act boldly on his assertion that the language of poetry should be "a selection of the real language of men," have clearly failed to please a large public. It would seem that in the eyes of their alienated readers, most poets of the last half-century or so have ceased to render significant shared or sharable experiences in an inspiring or illuminating way, instead becoming either the documenters of a fragmented world or the players of trivial word-games ("concrete poetry" being the *reductio ad absurdum*).

Before the rise of Romanticism, and vestigially long afterwards, "holding a mirror up to nature" meant elucidating a real order that existed below the surface of things. The unity of the poem reflected the unity of the world, something that the poetic imagination had found, not made. Thus Herrick in the seventeenth century described a traditionally prophetic view of the poet's function while remaining modest about his own pretensions to the afflatus:

'Tis not ev'ry day that I
Fitted am to prophesy;
No, but when the spirit fills
The fantastic pannicles
Full of fire, then I write
As the godhead doth indite.
Thus enraged, my lines are hurled,
Like the Sibyl's, through the world.
Look how next the holy fire
Either slakes, or doth retire;
So the fancy cools, till when
That brave spirit comes again.

Today the reflection of reality in poetry has come for many poets to mean the documentation of often meaningless details—frequently details of the poet's inner life—to demonstrate their meaninglessness or unintelligibility. This view of reality has led to a poetic content that is at the same time both trivial and presumptuous, while order in the poem has come to be seen as an artificial creation (often suspiciously so) rather than the form of discovery that is the poet's business.

Consequently, poets have largely abandoned heightened language and artificial meters in favor of everyday words and prose rhythms, an idiom Wordsworth may have suggested but was too prudent to carry very far. Since meter is the most obvious structural characteristic of all traditional poetry in English, the extent of its disuse today is surprising. Despite the fact that only three indisputably major figures in English have habitually used free verse—Whitman, Pound, and Eliot—it is now uncommon for a serious American poet to use anything else. The questionable assumption that traditional English meters are an anachronism in the contemporary world, and the even more dubious one that they should be replaced by the rhythms of everyday speech, have been dominant almost since the moment Pound began denouncing iambic pentameter. Those who do write in traditional meters, like Edgar Bowers, generally feel called upon to apologize for their backwardness. Only two poets in Mr. Heyen's selections use meter in any rigorous way; five more sometimes approximate it. Robert Frost in a famous exaggeration compared writing free verse to playing tennis without a net; he did not add that such a game might often be both tedious and confusing to watch. "The language is worn out," announced William Carlos Williams, a much more influential figure among recent poets. "I propose sweeping changes from top to bottom of the poetic structure." The persistence of rhyme and meter in poems written for children is a conspicuous survival and, no doubt, one reason why so many adults refuse to accept free verse as real poetry.

Both the kitchen-sink realism of so many twentieth-century poets and its opposite, the Wildean view that art has no relations with truth and teaches nothing, are further violations of what both the educated and the uneducated have always demanded of poetry. My impression is that relatively few contemporary poets (as opposed to critics) have altogether abandoned the ties between poetry and truth, although the modesty of poets' claims about the social impact of their art is understandably greater today than it has ever been. In contrast to Shelley's conception of poets as the unacknowledged legislators of the world, most living poets in England and America would probably agree, however ruefully, with Auden's humbler assertion that "poetry makes nothing happen." Like the insistence on realism of presentation, however, this attitude can be seen as representing a failure of confidence and purpose on the part of those poets who espouse it. Perhaps the most striking impression one gets from Mr. Heyen's twenty-nine essays is their authors' affectation of ordinariness, of being average confused citizens rather than seers or lawgivers. (In this unsurprising reaction to alienation, Williams was once again a leader.) Creeley, in many ways the most illuminating, complains about "the authoritative poetry of my youth."[10] But as literary historians are always reminding us, the poetry of Tennyson and Kipling did make things happen; so, in all likelihood, did that of Yeats, who feared in later life that he had aroused to arms "certain men the English shot."

The detailed documentation of society or the self is a task that can be most adequately undertaken by prose, film, and television. Poets are expected, however modestly, to make sense of life; if they find it in fragments they must not leave it that way. To do so is an abdication of duty and a failure of the shaping imagination, as nearly every poet from Homer to Chaucer to Keats would have accepted. In this minimal sense, at least, poets are still expected to be legislators and revealers of truth. The two most impressive twentieth-century poets, in this respect as in so many others, were probably Yeats and Frost. Rooted in backward regions of art and twentieth-century life, they shaped experience into insistent wholes that challenged the reader to reevaluate his own most important experiences and beliefs. No discerning reader has ever taken Frost's New England or Yeats's Ireland for real countries. Both are nations of the mind, conceived and presented with a vividness and coherence that make them illuminate the less realized countries that lie about us. Both poets had large audiences on all levels of sophistication except the very lowest.

The accurate, detailed reflection of everyday life in imaginative literature was a fashion that became a dogma among some writers and critics in the nineteenth century. It is probable, however, that the reading public's appetite for it came to be greatly overestimated. Such hunger for it as exists has been largely satisfied since the eighteenth century by prose fiction, a form that has little in common with poetry of any kind. Because the novel became prominent rather suddenly, at a particular time, its creators were free to experiment with it and impose on it such qualities as they wished, subject to the unformed tastes of a largely middle-class audience who wanted, among other things, a celebration in detail of their own hitherto largely unrecorded life. It is nonetheless worth noting that even in fiction, realistic modes are far less popular—and probably always have been—than such nonrealistic ones as the crime story, the romantic fantasy, the science-fiction novel.

That novelists have been free to produce such a variety of subforms, each with its own set of elaborate conventions, is an indication of the room for experimentation that a new and popular literary genre may offer its practitioners. (Ironically, subliterary prose fantasy—typically crime stories for men or romances for women—represents the highest achievement of autonomy in any form of writing. The work-as-object that bears the least possible relation to any reality outside itself is purchased in drugstores and at newsstands many thousands of times daily by a mass audience that never heard of the heresy of paraphrase.) Freedom to experiment within such broad limits has never existed for poets who wished to keep an audience, however, simply because poetry has existed longer than the modern world. The public has *known* for so long what poetry is, and its ideas about poetic purposes have been so often and powerfully reinforced by anthologists in the tradition of Palgrave, that the efforts of modern poets who wished to adapt it to what they saw as the requirements of modern civilization have met with little enthusiasm among readers. Pound, Eliot, Auden, and their successors have largely had their way on English-language poetry in the last fifty years—the modern poems taught in universities (pace McKuen) and discussed in critical journals are almost entirely their recognizable offspring—but at the cost of alienating most of the audience that remained for serious poetry at the turn of the century, and without creating a new one, except for the temporarily captive student.

To blame the public for being old-fashioned in its demands, or for having low tastes, is an inadequate response to such a striking literary phenomenon as the disaster that has befallen poetry in this century. It is obvious that the people who have made Rod McKuen such a comfort to his publishers show abysmal taste, but it is also arguable that McKuen flourishes in part because he has little living competition—because people who make traditional demands on poetry really have few better alternatives. The complaint that the contemporary public (educated or not) wants Victorian kinds of "authoritative" poetry is perhaps more enlightening. The relative popularity of Sir John Betjeman in both England and America suggests that a large public does like verse that has rhyme and meter—the accepted forms by which language in English poetry has been heightened, set apart from prose, and made memorable—and that energetically presents a clear point of view. It is doubtful that at any time in the past many people have read poetry entirely for esthetic pleasure; nor did any major literary critic before the mid-nineteenth century suggest that readers should have to choose between beauty and truth. Whether or not they actually believe or do what poets tell them, most people have always expected poetry to illuminate some significant aspect of life, in lines that stick in the mind. To ridicule this demand because it has sometimes inspired pompous verse is to dismiss one of poetry's major historic functions.

Since the levels of taste represented by popular poets like McKuen are likely to be outgrown by anyone of normal intelligence, the existing poetic audience today is probably younger than it has ever been. Whereas a sensitive late-Victorian teenager might have graduated from Henley and Newbolt to Hardy and Housman, his present-day equivalent has nothing to move up to that he is apt to recognize as poetry unless he majors in English at a university; he is therefore almost certain to stop reading poetry, or at least poetry by living authors, by the age of thirty, unless his mental development is arrested at an earlier age. The great-grandchildren of the people who bought the works of Tennyson, Browning, and Longfellow do not, most of them, buy any new works of poetry today. Whether *their* great-grandchildren will buy any may depend on whether poets in the next generation or two can throw off those parts of the modernist legacy that are dead weight and return to a more traditional conception of the forms and functions of poetry without simply producing parodies of the poetry written in previous centuries. Despite the cultural changes that are the theme of this book, it should be possible—it should always have been possible— to produce a twentieth-century poetry that is recognizably different from that of the nineteenth without abandoning what the audience had always been led to believe poetry was. To say that the twentieth century required the literary discontinuities that the modernists and post-modernists imposed on it is to exaggerate grossly the differences between human nature and needs in this age as against all previous ones. How and why a style, a genre, a given author or work becomes fashionable is an important and inadequately studied question in literary history. The reasons for the current unfashionableness of serious poetry with its natural audiences are not far to seek; nor, alas, are the reasons for the fashionableness of contemporary academic poetry (much of it pretending to be anti-academic) with its own tiny audience of alienated literary scholars. They are, in essence, the same reasons.

In its early days as a valiant purveyor of modernism, *Poetry* magazine carried on its cover a quotation from Whitman: "To have great poets, there must be great audiences too." A major failing that unites many British and American poets from Pound onwards is their lack of perceptiveness about the real or potential audience and what it might value in poetry during a century like ours. Pound's quest for the ideal reader who could understand both Greek and Chinese and who also knew the smallest details of the poet's private life was a dead end, and an ironic one for a poet who had once preached the use of everyday language and materials. Instead of the two-level public—us and them—that the modernists came to assume, it might be more accurate and fruitful to posit four or five levels, several of which are worth aiming at. The partly philistine audience of Victorian poetry could never have been as potent a source of demoralization to poets as having virtually no audience at all.

The probable desire of twentieth-century readers and potential readers of poetry for coherence, memorableness, and even inspiration ought not to be dismissed as escapism or superficial optimism. It may on the contrary be a desire for help in defeating a perceived malaise—a desire for a socially important literature that transcends or illuminates the ills of modern life rather than an isolated literature that helplessly mirrors them. Messages, as we have seen, need be neither shallow nor pretentiously cosmic. The rise of science to intellectual hegemony in the modern world did not inevitably doom to extinction poetic discourse and the figurative kinds of insight it represented. It might in the long run even have made them more precious to a world that was being hustled along by technology in directions that few readers were conscious of having willed for themselves. As the century progressed and the consequences of science came to seem increasingly ominous, the public's disillusionment with the dominant modes of understanding and managing the world might have posed a genuine opportunity for poets whose confidence and sense of purpose had prepared them to take advantage of it. But by the last third of the century, poets had been isolated for so long—neither prophets nor paid entertainers—that their morale seemed nearly irrecoverable, and most of them saw in the increasing troubles of science and technology merely reason for withdrawing even more deeply from a civilization that had, they thought, rejected poets irrevocably.

"I will friend you, if I may, / In the dark and cloudy day," wrote Housman, who had a large audience, in the poem that summed up the purposes of his art. That art was for the communication of exceptional experience, perception, and emotion, all together, in language that immediately signalled itself to the dullest reader as distinct from prose.

Such a promise might have been made, although in different ways, by both the sophisticated and the popular poetry of the past. Today the only large body of verse that has apparently been faithful to traditional conceptions, and has therefore kept its audience, is the least sophisticated. Insofar as serious artists will not provide such rewards of friendship, the audience will naturally either disappear or gravitate to non-art—to pulp fiction, to the half-hour television programs that are the major forms of drama in our time, to rock music and Rod McKuen. To treat this situation merely as proof of bad taste blinds one to the fact that it is also evidence of paralysis or abdication among artists.[11]

Writing recently in the *Hudson Review,* Wendell Berry attributes that paralysis in large part to what he calls the "specialization" of contemporary poetry. Despite the more political poetry of the 1960s, he declares, "Poetry remains a specialized art, its range and influence so constricted that poets have very nearly become their own audience." Poets, he goes on, have cut themselves off from both the traditions of their art and the world of ordinary experience. "Isolated by the specialization of their art—by their tendency to make a religion of poetry or to make a world out of words, and by their preoccupation with the present and the new—poets of modern times seem to run extreme occupational risks."[12] What he misses, I think, is one of the paradoxes I have been talking about—that the privateness and lack of power that we both complain of has some of its roots in sterile forms of realism, in the aspiration to mirror the modern world and what was presumed to be the modern self more faithfully than poetry had done before, directly or with the aid of forgotten myths. Pound, the early Eliot, Williams, the later Lowell—all would have subscribed to such an ideal. It is a sad fact that, for the last seventy years, the waste land really has looked to many poets like the promised land.

It might be argued against either Berry's indictment or mine, of course, that to subsume all or most modern poetry under such a series of generalizations is to ignore its variousness ("healthy variety" to those who approve, "fragmentation" to those who do not). And indeed, an age in which there are no longer any generally accepted standards of poetic taste or merit will inevitably produce a great variety of poetic intentions and achievements, some of them admirable. To speak only of contemporary poets, A.D. Hope and John Hollander have (in different ways) made praiseworthy applications of seventeenth-century form and tradition to modern subjects. Derek Walcott, one of the most notable regionalists writing today, has effectively married a Yeatsian formal elegance with West Indian materials, while Judith Wright's combination of precision and emotional intensity makes one regret that she is not better known outside Australia. Even Robert Bly's sometimes eccentric blend of nature-mysticism and new-left politics is, at its best, a constructive attempt to reinterest a contemporary audience in poetry by maintaining traditional kinds of poetic significance. Examples could be multiplied of such attempts in the English-speaking world over the last two or three decades. But the fact remains that all twentieth-century poets in English have come up against the transformations in Anglo-American civilization that have taken place since science began to change people's ways of thinking and living, and none have found a successful way of reintroducing poetry into the mainstream of culture. In the very act of seeking poetic responses to these changes, they have, on balance, merely deepened their own solitude.

Like poets today, the first generation of Romantics found themselves faced with two questions that involved the very survival of their art. The first, according to W.J. Bate, was the stark query posed by their predecessors' intimidating and varied achievement over many centuries: *What is there left to do?* The second question was whether, given the vast cultural changes that were taking place around them, it was still possible for poets to gain and hold a significant audience in an age whose leading prophets were already proclaiming the death of poetry. The ways the Romantics devised of answering these questions gave poetry a lease on life that no dispassionate observer in 1798 would have been likely to predict. "To an important extent," Bate declares, "that 'rescue' of the arts through the extension of their public did happen, against all the theoretical probabilities, and was to continue to happen throughout the nineteenth century." Romanticism brought about a sustained revival of serious poetry that appealed to a broad audience, thereby mitigating to an impressive degree not only the alienation of the artist that was itself to become a theme of Romantic art, but also the dehumanizing effects of nineteenth-century industrial and scientific progress. If the poetry of the Romantics and Victorians did not quite succeed as prophecy in visionary terms, it nevertheless bore indispensable witness to the liberating power of the imagination in a discouraging time, a witness for which the reading public in England and America were properly grateful.

By its very success in preserving an honorable place for poetry, however, Romanticism augmented for the succeeding century the same difficulties it had itself faced at its beginnings, leaving early-twentieth-century poets to ask anew the same two questions under even more trying circumstances.

> For the romantic effort, with its remarkable if emotionally specialized success, was to create an immense problem for the twentieth century in its own traumatic attempt to disengage itself from the nineteenth. Forced to establish and defend a difference, the twentieth century was led into a situation where . . . it often found itself compelled to champion the anti-popular (humanly confusing the "*anti*-popular" with the merely "a-popular" or the "unpopular"), without either wanting to do so or quite knowing why it was doing so.[13]

The result, to a considerable degree, was the modernists' half-deliberate alienation of the audience that poets a century earlier had taken such pains to create.

Seven decades have now passed since the first rattling gunfire of the modernist revolution, a longer period than had then elapsed since the death of Wordsworth, and it is reasonable to ask whether the kind of rescue operation the Romantics performed for English poetry is possible a second time. To raise such a question may be a suitable way of ending this exploration of poetry's decline, even though no answer to it is possible. For in two centuries we have in many ways come full circle, and the late afternoon of the scientific age—if that indeed is where we are—may be no more unpromising a time for poetry than its dawning was. The need for poetry, as I have already suggested, is not less in an era like ours than in any other, contrary to the impression that many twentieth-century poets and their potential readers have conspired to create. The reading public is larger and more restless than ever before, while the cultural fixities of the last century and a half look frailer than they did even a decade ago. The opportunities that the end of the twentieth century offers to poetry will not become fully apparent unless and until poets take advantage of them, but it would be foolishly pessimistic to maintain that there are no opportunities at all.

The recovery of the balance between thought, feeling, and form, and of a more fruitful sense of subjects and purposes, will not alone restore poetry to its rightful place; as always, many important factors are beyond the control of poets. Nevertheless, I conclude by suggesting, as one of the chief implications of this book, that the effort of such a recovery would be a good start. The time is long past when any poet needs to assert his distinctness from his nineteenth-century forebears, and it would be very surprising if some of the positive ideals of modernism—the use of myth, a sophisticated regionalism, a more precise poetic language than was usual in the nineteenth century—did not show up somewhere in such a balance. As every period of literature and civilization demonstrates, repudiating one's spiritual and intellectual predecessors wholesale is no more profitable than imitating them slavishly. If the poetry of the future rises to its challenges, it will bear the features of all its ancestors and at the same time be something new and unique, an achievement whose outlines no critic can possibly hope to predict.

NOTES

ONE: Rhyme or Reason

1. Gémino H. Abad, *A Formal Approach to Lyric Poetry* (Quezon City: Univ. of the Philippines, 1978), 130.

2. C. Hugh Holman, *A Handbook to Literature,* Third Edition (Indianapolis: Bobbs-Merrill, 1972), s.v. *Poetry.*

3. Samuel Johnson, *Lives of the English Poets,* ed. G.B. Hill (Oxford: Clarendon Press, 1905), 3:251.

4. Barbara Hardy, *The Advantage of Lyric* (Bloomington: Indiana Univ. Press, 1977), 1, 2.

5. Sir Philip Sidney, *Defence of Poetry* (London: Macmillan, 1963), 8.

6. Yvor Winters, *Forms of Discovery* (Chicago: Alan Swallow, 1967), xiv, xix.

7. F.H. Anderson, *The Philosophy of Francis Bacon* (New York: Octagon, 1975), 149-53; *The Works of Francis Bacon,* ed. James Spedding *et al.* (London: Longman, 1860), 4:314-18.

8. John Locke, *An Essay Concerning Human Understanding,* ed. Peter H. Nidditch (Oxford: Clarendon, 1975), 508.

9. George Watson, *The Literary Critics* (Harmondsworth: Penguin, 1973), 5.

10. David Cecil, "Thomas Gray," in *Poets and Story-Tellers* (London: Constable, 1949), 49.

11. *The Works of Thomas Love Peacock,* ed. H.F.B. Brett-Smith and C.E. Jones (London: Constable, 1924), 8:9.

12. *The Complete Works of Lord Macaulay,* ed. Lady Trevelyan (New York: Longmans Green, 1898), 1:5-7.

13. Charles Darwin, *Autobiography,* ed. Nora Barlow (New York: Norton, 1969), 139.

14. M.H. Abrams, *The Mirror and the Lamp* (New York: Oxford, 1969), 313-15.

15. Yvor Winters, *The Function of Criticism* (Denver: Alan Swallow, 1957), 104.

16. *The Works of Matthew Arnold* (London: Macmillan, 1903), 3:5-6.

17. George Watson, *The Study of Literature* (New York: Scribner, 1969), 200-202.

18. Lionel Trilling, *The Liberal Imagination* (New York: Doubleday, 1957), 278, 280.

19. Ronald S. Crane, "Philosophy, Literature and the History of Ideas," in *The Idea of the Humanities* (Chicago: Univ. of Chicago Press, 1967), 1:187.

20. W.H. Auden, *The Dyer's Hand* (New York: Vintage, 1968), 26.

Two: Poetry as Revelation

1. I omit Coleridge because of his comparatively traditional Christianity, though he obviously contributed to the set of ideas I am discussing. Blake, who may seem today a more thorough and effective prophet than Wordsworth, is missing for another reason: as a poet he was largely ignored in the nineteenth century.

2. Eric Havelock, *Preface to Plato* (Cambridge, Mass.: Harvard, 1963), 6. The discussion that develops on the following pages is heavily indebted to Havelock's study, which examines the attack on poets at length. For a somewhat different reading of Plato's attitude toward poets, one that relies heavily on the *Phaedrus,* see Eric Voegelin, *Plato and Aristotle* (Baton Rouge: Louisiana State Univ. Press, 1957), esp. 138-39.

3. *The Works of Jeremy Bentham* (Bowring edition, reprinted New York: Russell and Russell, 1962), 2:253-54.

4. *Shelley's Poetry and Prose,* ed. Donald H. Reiman and S.B. Powers (New York: Norton, 1977), 480. All subsequent references are to this edition, which is based on the manuscript that Shelley approved for publication.

5. *The Works of Thomas Carlyle,* ed. H.D. Traill (London: Chapman and Hall, 1897), 5:80.

6. John Stuart Mill, "Thoughts on Poetry and Its Varieties" (1833), in *Essays on Poetry by John Stuart Mill,* ed. F. Parrin Sharpless (Columbia, S.C.: Univ. of South Carolina Press, 1976), 5-6. The literature on Mill and poetry is enormous; see, *inter alia,* Thomas Woods, *Poetry and Philosophy* (London: Hutchinson, 1961) and Edward Alexander, *Matthew Arnold and John Stuart Mill* (New York: Columbia, 1965).

7. *Works,* 4:2.

8. James Benziger, *Images of Eternity* (Carbondale: Southern Illinois Univ. Press, 1962), 222.

9. *Works,* 4:338-39.

10. Lionel Trilling, in his *Matthew Arnold* (New York: Harcourt Brace, 1978), makes the same point somewhat differently: "Here is poetic experience merely, and however much the poetic experience may order our lives, however much pseudo-statement may organize our emotions, its effect is not so great as that of 'statement' or what we firmly believe to be statement" (365). I.A. Richards' *Science and Poetry* (1926), which popularized the term "pseudo-statement," has been revised and republished under the title *Poetries and Sciences* (New York: Norton, 1970).

11. *The Complete Works of Edgar Allan Poe,* ed. James A. Harrison (New York: G.D. Sproul, 1902), 14:271-72.

12. Or, as Donald Hall puts it in *Remembering Poets* (New York: Harper and Row, 1978), "Poetry exists to extend human consciousness, to bring materials and insights from the unconscious dark into the light of language. . . . We must add the thesis of pre-verbal, irrational thinking to the antithesis of secondary rationalism. . . . All poets have dictator Plato inside themselves, attempting repression of the internal Orpheus" (196-97).

13. Robert Duncan, *The Truth and Life of Myth* (Fremont, Mich.: Sumac Press, 1968), 22, 25.

THREE: The Land of Lost Content

1. The sentimental image of the child as a pure, spiritual creature owes much to Evangelical propaganda around 1800. See Samuel Pickering, *The Moral Tradition in English Fiction* (Hanover, N.H.: Univ. Press of New England, 1976), chapter one. On the development of the theme, see Peter Coveney, *Poor Monkey: The Child in Literature* (London: Rockliff, 1957) and Robert Pattison, *The Child Figure in English Literature* (Athens: Univ. of Georgia Press, 1978).

2. I say "at least in theory" to accommodate Frost's "Directive" and Dylan Thomas's "Fern Hill," which were published four and five years respectively after "Little Gidding"; but of course neither poet was English.

3. I am purposely ignoring "Intimations of Immortality" because the way in which childhood is there idealized is significantly different. No doubt the emotional need is the same, but "clouds of glory" are so unlike "glad animal movements" that we become confused (or even deceived) about just what it is that was so important in childhood. Of course the "Intimations" view of children had a respectable history; but the neoplatonic disguise did not really fit the impulse (at least in our period), and we do not see it again in major poetry, except perhaps in Yeats. The major religious point about Victorian nostalgia for childhood is that children are innocent and pre-theological, while doctrines are a misguided creation of the adult mind. For similar reasons one can ignore Wordsworth's debts to the eighteenth-century graveyard school in this context; when they went to churchyards they were looking for something quite different from what Wordsworth and his successors sought.

4. In other poems with a less evolutionary bent, Tennyson complies much more agreeably with the Wordsworthian attitude. The last parts of "The Two Voices," for example, are altogether Wordsworthian in their attitudes toward both childhood and nature, and even take place outside the obligatory church. But it seems to me more revealing to look at his *major* poem from this standpoint. Those who wish to regard *Idylls of the King* as a more important statement than *In Memoriam* will probably reject my approach.

5. Joseph Warren Beach, *The Concept of Nature in Nineteenth-Century English Poetry* (New York: Macmillan, 1936), especially part 3.

6. It is worth remembering that Ruskin, a very different Victorian, underwent a very different spiritual commotion at the Grande Chartreuse in 1849, which he recounts in the third volume of *Praeterita*.

FOUR: The Palgrave Version

1. Because the definition of *lyric* today is a vexed question—thanks largely to the victory of the lyric over all other poetic forms—and the word's connotations so

powerful, Yvor Winters chose to employ instead the term *short poem* in his history of the form. While I agree that for these reasons *short poem* is preferable, Palgrave used *lyric* and therefore so shall I in discussing him.

2. W.B. Yeats, *Essays and Introductions* (New York: Macmillan, 1961), 491.

3. Naomi Lewis, "Palgrave and His 'Golden Treasury'," *Listener,* 67 (1961), 23.

4. *The Golden Treasury,* First Edition (Cambridge and London: Macmillan, 1861), preface (which has unnumbered pages). All quotations from *The Golden Treasury* are from this edition; page numbers will be cited in the text.

5. Lewis, "Palgrave and His 'Golden Treasury'," 23.

6. Gwennlian F. Palgrave, ed., *Francis Turner Palgrave: His Journals and Memories of His Life* (London: Longmans Green, 1899), 73.

7. Evelyn Hardy, *Thomas Hardy: A Critical Biography* (London: Hogarth, 1954) , 52. See also Robert Gittings, *Young Thomas Hardy* (London: Heinemann, 1975), 56.

8. Henry Maas, ed., *Letters of A.E. Housman* (Cambridge, Mass.: Harvard, 1971), 41; P.A. Larkin, "Palgrave's Last Anthology: A.E. Housman's Copy," *Rev. of English Studies,* 22 (1971), 312-16.

9. *The Oxford Book of English Verse* (Oxford: Clarendon, 1925), ix-x. (First published 1900.)

10. "Francis Turner Palgrave," in *The Penguin Companion to English Literature* (Harmondsworth: Penguin, 1971), 411. Colin Horne makes what is perhaps the same point very differently: "Like Arnold, though more gently, Palgrave sought to convert the Philistine and to enlighten the newly literate masses." ("Palgrave's *Golden Treasury,*" *English Studies,* 2 [1949], 54.)

11. Matthew Arnold, "The Study of Poetry," in *Works,* 4:2.

12. Walter Pater, "Style," in *Appreciations, With an Essay on Style* (London: Macmillan, 1910), 10.

13. W.B. Yeats, *Autobiographies* (London: Macmillan, 1955), 115.

14. T.H. Huxley, "On Science and Art in Relation to Education," in *Collected Essays* (New York: Appleton, 1898), 3:179.

15. Gwennlian F. Palgrave, *Journals and Memories,* 65.

16. Murray Prosky, "Lamb, Palgrave, and the Elizabethans in T.S. Eliot's *The Waste Land,*" *Studies in the Humanities,* 2 (Fall-Winter 1970-71), 11-16.

17. Palgrave made the same point in "The Growth of English Poetry," a long essay published three months after *The Golden Treasury*: "We would sum up the contrast of the old and new by saying that poetry is now an instrument of greater depth, finish, and compass . . . poetry speaks a more universal language and gives back the age to itself with a completer utterance, than in the days of Allegory, and Pastoral, and Drama." (*Quarterly Review,* 220 [October 1861], 452.)

18. Francis T. Palgrave, *The Children's Treasury of Lyrical Poetry* (London: Macmillan, 1909), vii.

19. *The Golden Treasury: Second Series* (New York: Macmillan, 1898), ix.

20. Horne, "Palgrave's *Golden Treasury,*" 62-63.

21. Quoted in Joseph Hone, *W.B. Yeats* (London: Macmillan, 1965), 394.

FIVE: New Bottles

1. "The Metaphysical Poets," in *Selected Prose of T.S. Eliot,* ed. Frank Kermode (New York: Harcourt, Brace, 1975), 65.

2. Linda Wagner, *Interviews with William Carlos Williams* (New York: New Directions, 1976), 63, 59, 71.

3. Laura Riding and Robert Graves, *A Survey of Modernist Poetry* (London: Heinemann, 1927), 178-79. For a sympathetic history of poetic modernism that puts Pound at the centre, see Hugh Kenner, *The Pound Era* (Berkeley: Univ. of California, 1971); for a broader history of poetry in English from the late nineteenth century until the 1920s, see David Perkins, *A History of Modern Poetry: From the Eighteen-Nineties to the High Modernist Mode* (Cambridge, Mass.: Harvard, 1976).

4. T.S. Eliot, *After Strange Gods* (New York: Harcourt, Brace, 1934), 30.

5. M.L. Rosenthal, *Sailing Into the Unknown* (New York: Oxford, 1978), 205.

6. T.S. Eliot, review of John Middleton Murry's biography of D.H. Lawrence, *Criterion,* 10 (1931), 769.

7. Walt Whitman, "A Backward Glance O'er Travel'd Roads," in *Leaves of Grass,* ed. Sculley Bradley and Harold W. Blodgett (New York: Norton, 1973), 564.

8. T.S. Eliot, "Ulysses, Order and Myth," in *Selected Prose,* 178.

9. Cyril Connolly, *The Unquiet Grave* (New York: Viking, 1957), 120-21.

10. Riding and Graves, *Modernist Poetry,* 277.

11. T.S. Eliot, "Religion and Literature," in *Selected Prose,* 104.

SIX: Grecian Thoughts in the Home Fields

1. Donald Davidson, "The Artist as Southerner," *Saturday Review of Literature,* 15 May 1926, 781-82. Like Ransom and Tate, of course, Davidson had considerably moderated his criticism by the time of his contribution to *I'll Take My Stand.*

2. That it also served other purposes unrelated to the question of regionalism I am not, of course, denying. It goes without saying that, as with the other Fugitives, there are many important aspects of Ransom's mind and art that fall outside my subject.

3. If Warren is ultimately accepted as a major twentieth-century poet—and his recent productivity makes any judgment on his career as a whole tentative—perhaps his general movement away from regional subjects has been a factor in his evolution to that status. Such a change of focus may not represent a very important loss outside the present context, but it reinforces my contention that Southern poets have had a hard time writing effectively about the South.

4. "I use Narcissism to mean only preoccupation with self; it may be either love or hate," says Tate in "Narcissus as Narcissus" (1936), reprinted in *The Man of Letters in the Modern World* (New York: Meridian, 1955), 335. Since the speaker of the poem is given no specific characterization or relationships, it is difficult to say whether he is really preoccupied with himself in the way that, for example, Prufrock is.

5. Tate: "All the tests of its success in style and versification would come in the end to a single test, an answer, yes or no, to the question: Assuming that the Confederates and Narcissus are not yoked together by mere violence, has the poet convinced the reader that, on the specific occasion of this poem, there is a necessary yet hitherto undetected relation between them?" ("Narcissus as Narcissus," 336.)

6. John Tyree Fain and Thomas Daniel Young, eds., *The Literary Correspondence of Donald Davidson and Allen Tate* (Athens: Univ. of Georgia, 1974), 186.

7. Undated letter in the Vanderbilt Collection, quoted in *Georgia Review,* 27 (1973), 555.

8. "I am beginning to see myself as Ransom's Captain Carpenter," Davidson wrote Tate on 2 March 1938.

9. John Crowe Ransom, "Modern with the Southern Accent," *Virginia Quarterly Review,* 11 (1935), 199-200.

10. *American Review,* 8 December 1936, 142-50.

SEVEN: The Place of Poetry

1. W. Jackson Bate, *The Burden of the Past and the English Poet* (Cambridge, Mass.: Belknap, 1970), 119.

2. S.I. Hayakawa, *Language in Thought and Action,* Second Edition (New York: Harcourt, Brace, 1964), 268, 269.

3. Richard Jones, "Scottish and Welsh Nationalism," *Virginia Quarterly Review,* 54 (1978), 49.

4. Most, but not all. See Joseph Bruchas, *The Poetry of Pop* (Paradise, Calif.: Dustbooks, 1973), for a variety of criticism of which we may expect to see much more. Anyone who teaches literature to undergraduates today knows that many of them regard Bob Dylan and John Denver as the most important twentieth-century poets. Alas, there are plenty of professors willing to encourage them in this belief.

5. Bate, *Burden of the Past,* 120.

6. Riding and Graves, *Modernist Poetry,* 84.

7. William Heyen, ed., *American Poets in 1976* (Indianapolis: Bobbs-Merrill, 1976), 97.

8. Delmore Schwartz, "The Isolation of Modern Poetry," quoted in Steven K. Hoffman, "Impersonal Personalism: The Making of a Confessional Poetic," *ELH,* 45 (1978), 688.

9. Wagner, *Interviews with William Carlos Williams,* 74; Heyen, *American Poets,* 51.

10. Heyen, *American Poets,* 46.

11. As W.H. Auden points out, the distinction between sophisticated art and popular art no longer exists; the latter has been completely swallowed up by the entertainment industry, whose purposes and products are not artistic at all. "This is bad for everyone," Auden says; "the majority lose all genuine taste of their own, and the minority become cultural snobs" (*The Dyer's Hand,* 83).

12. Wendell Berry, "The Specialization of Poetry" (1975), reprinted in Reginald

Gibbons, ed., *The Poet's Work* (Boston: Houghton Mifflin, 1979), 140, 149. Gerald Graff's *Literature Against Itself* (Chicago: Univ. of Chicago Press, 1979) appeared just as I was completing this book. Since Graff and I are in close agreement on so many questions, it may strike anyone who reads both books as odd that while I criticize contemporary poetry for being too realistic, he attacks contemporary literature in general for precisely the opposite failing. The reason for this bizarre divergence is, I think, twofold: we are perhaps talking about different writers (Graff's main concern being with fiction), and his use of the term *realism* is different from mine. I suspect that his expressed desire for realistic or "mimetic" literature is really for a literature that does not simply reproduce reality (however conceived) but criticizes it from some normative standpoint.

13. Bate, *Burden of the Past,* 3, 121-22.

INDEX

Abad, Gémino H., 3, 22
Abrams, M. H., 17-18, 34
Allen, Hervey, 114
Ammons, A. R., 114
Aristotle, 72
Arnold, Matthew, 17, 49, 53-55, 89, 91, 96; defends poetry, 40-44; defines poetry, 21; *Empedocles on Etna*, 54, 70; "Function of Criticism," 22-23; "Stanzas from the Grande Chartreuse," 54-55
Auden, W. H., 26, 85, 120, 126, 128, 140 n.11

Bacon, Sir Francis, 8
Bailey, Philip James: *Festus*, 29
Bate, Walter Jackson, 118, 122, 132, 133
Beach, Joseph Warren, 53
Bentham, Jeremy, 5, 33, 34, 40
Berry, Wendell, 131
Betjeman, Sir John, 128
Blake, William, 18, 19, 46, 136 n.1
Bly, Robert, 132
Bowers, Edgar, 126
Brooks, Cleanth, 109
Browning, Robert: *The Ring and the Book*, 66, 70

Camus, Albert, 108
Carlyle, Thomas, 37-39
Cecil, Lord David, 10
Civil War, the (American), 108-9

Coleridge, Samuel Taylor, 3-4, 40, 136 n.1
Connolly, Cyril, 94
Crane, Ronald, 24-25
Creeley, Robert, 124, 126

Dante, 29
Darwin, Charles, 16, 17, 58, 72; *Origin of Species*, 37
Davidson, Donald, 102-4, 116; "Lee in the Mountains," 109, 111-13; "Sanctuary," 112
Denver, John, 140 n.4
Dickey, James, 101
Dickinson, Emily, 3, 4, 19-20
Donne, John, 30
Doolittle, Hilda ("H. D."), 84; *The Walls Do Not Fall*, 96
Duncan, Robert, 46-47, 91
Dylan, Bob, 140 n.4

Eliot, Thomas Stearns, 44-46 *passim*, 58-62, 116, 125, 128, 131; and Modernism, 83-96 *passim*; "Burnt Norton," 59; *Four Quartets*, 96; "Little Gidding," 49, 60-62, 90; "Prufrock," 80; *The Waste Land*, 46, 59, 76-77, 91
Esthetic Movement, 21, 70-71

Faulkner, William, 100
Fletcher, John Gould, 111
Frost, Robert, 21, 72, 100, 116, 126, 127
Fugitives, the, 99-103 *passim*, 115

Quiller-Couch, Sir Arthur, 68

Ransom, John Crowe, 100, 101, 114,
  139 n.2; "Antique Harvesters,"
  104-5; "Dead Boy," 103; "Old
  Mansion," 103, 104
Richards, I. A., 44, 136 n.10
Riding, Laura, 96; *Survey of Modernist
  Poetry*, 86-88, 95, 122-23
Robinson, Edwin Arlington, 4
Romanticism, 79, 124, 132, 133
Rosenthal, M. L., 89, 90, 91
Ross, Angus, 69
Ruskin, John: *Modern Painters*, 67,
  137 n.6

Schwartz, Delmore, 124
Scott, Sir Walter: "The Pride of
  Youth," 75
Shakespeare, William, 38-39
Shelley, Percy Bysshe, 8, 12, 30, 69,
  126; *Defence of Poetry*, 34-37
Sidney, Sir Philip, 5, 6, 8, 9, 10, 25
Southern regionalism, 97-117
Stevens, Wallace, 85, 95

Tate, Allen, 100-102, 105, 116,
  140 n.5; "Ode to the Confederate
  Dead," 109-12
Tennyson, Alfred, Lord, 41, 49, 69,
  126; *Idylls of the King*, 66, 70,

137 n.4; *In Memoriam*, 51, 52-53,
  66, 70, 72; "The Two Voices,"
  137 n.4
Trilling, Lionel, 23-24, 136 n.10

Walcott, Derek, 132
Warren, Robert Penn, 100, 101, 112,
  115, 116, 139 n.3; "The Ballad of
  Billie Potts," 105, 106-8, 111
Watson, George, 10, 23
Whitman, Walt, 18, 41, 91-94
  passim, 125, 129
Wilbur, Richard, 120
Williams, William Carlos, 18, 84,
  85, 93, 95, 124, 126, 131;
  Paterson, 96
Wilson, Edmund, 99, 100, 102
Winters, Yvor, 7, 20, 21, 137-38 n.1
Wordsworth, William, 5, 69, 75,
  125; and loss of childhood, 48,
  49-51, 53, 56, 60, 124; on poetry,
  3; and poetry as revelation, 28-30,
  43; "Intimations Ode," 24, 78,
  137 n.3; *The Prelude*, 23, 24, 49,
  66; "Tintern Abbey," 29, 49
Wright, Judith, 132
Wyse, Lois, 121

Yeats, William Butler, 45, 66, 71,
  82-103 *passim*, 116, 126, 127,
  137 n.3; "Adam's Curse," 93